St DAVID

THE OFFICIAL ANNIVERSARY BOOK OF STENA LINE

FISHGUARD ROSSLARE

1906-2006

Compiled by Miles Cowsill

CONTRIBUTORS:

Dick Clague
Richard Kirkman
Martin Lewis
Robert Lloyd
John Maddock
Bernard Share
Gareth Williams

Stena Line
Making good time™

Published by:
Ferry Publications, PO Box 33, Ramsey, Isle of Man IM99 4LP
Tel: +44 (0) 1624 898445 Fax: +44 (0) 1624 898449
E-mail: FerryPubs@manx.net Website: www.ferrypubs.co.uk

FISHGUARD ROSSLARE

CONTENTS

Published by Ferry Publications Ltd
PO Box 33, Ramsey, Isle of Man,
British Isles, IM99 4LP
Tel: +44 (0) 1624 898445 Fax: +44 (0) 1624 898449
E Mail: ferrypubs@manx.net

Published: June 2006

INTRODUCTION

Between 1962 and 1977, living in Kent, I saw rapid development of Dover's ferry industry. In 1978 I moved to Pembrokeshire – a decision which proved to be equally enlightening, giving me the opportunity to witness the dawn of a similarly exciting new era for the growing Welsh ferry port of Fishguard (which incidentally is the closest British port to New York).

The move also provided the chance for me to cross the Irish Sea aboard the graceful *Avalon*. She was in her twilight years of operation, having been converted to a car ferry in 1974 following her earlier distinguished service on the Harwich-Hook of Holland route and her off-season cruising in Europe. Within 18 months of my move she was retired from service.

My first Fishguard-to-Rosslare sailing on the *Avalon* was memorable – in stark contrast to the Dover vessels I was used to, such as *Hengist, Chartres* and the series of very modern vessels in the Free Enterprise class built by Townsend Thoresen. Not only was the vessel so different from my previous experiences of ferry travel; both ports were nothing like the sprawling complexes of Dover's Eastern Docks and Calais.

Fishguard at the time was served by a regular and well patronised direct train service from Paddington (usually hauled by a Class 37 or Class 47 diesel), and the Rosslare of 1978 was a far cry from the port it is today. Temporary buildings served as ferry booking offices and other terminal facilities, there was only one linkspan, and a wonderful rickety old red bus conveyed passengers from the gang-plank to the station.

At the end of the 1970s, rapid and radical change came to these ports, the ships and the route, starting in 1979. Peter Fenton, then General Manager of the port of Fishguard, convinced Sealink management in London to charter the Swedish-registered vessel *Stena Normandica*, which was designed to carry large numbers of freight lorries and cars, and for the next ten years she was an overwhelming success.

By 1990 the growth in freight traffic on the Irish Sea demanded even greater capacity, and another Swedish-registered ship, the *Stena Felicity*, replaced her. The route's next development was the introduction of the fast-ferry service on St George's Channel. This opened the day-trip market on both

The graceful **Avalon** *comes astern at Rosslare following her conversion to a car ferry in 1978. (Ferry Publications Library)*

The current vessel on the Fishguard-Rosslare service is the **Stena Europe**. *She is seen here swinging off the berth at Fishguard in September 2005 on her regular afternoon crossing to Ireland. (Miles Cowsill)*

sides of the Irish Sea and enabled the route to compete with its central corridor counterpart of Sealink, who had already initiated their own fast-ferry route between Holyhead and Dun Laoghaire.

1997 saw the arrival of *Koningin Beatrix* – possibly the most luxuriously-appointed vessel ever to enter service on the route – and the subsequent removal of the *Stena Felicity*, followed in 2002 by the introduction of the *Stena Europe*.

Today, 27 years on, the market is very different from when I set up home in Pembrokeshire. Road communications between port and capital city have improved dramatically on each side of St George's Channel, and both Fishguard and Rosslare terminals have benefited greatly from similar significant advances during the last ten years.

The port of Fishguard now boasts four linkspans and handles over 590,000 passengers a year. Although passenger rail traffic has dropped considerably since the 1980s, freight traffic has grown beyond all expectations – a trend likely to continue as Ireland and Britain, strong EU members, further their flourishing trade links.

Crucial though it is to focus on the future, it is a sobering thought that none of this would have been possible had it not been for those brave Victorian entrepreneurs who put their money and faith into Fishguard. The idea of constructing the port today, from scratch, would be dismissed as a totally unviable proposition.

The same historical perspective applies equally to Rosslare, which was established despite severe and determined opposition by many who could not see the benefits of such a far-sighted project. Today Rosslare is one of the key ports of Ireland, serving the UK and France with up to 35 departures weekly at the height of the season.

On a personal note, it has been a great pleasure to produce this 100th anniversary book for Stena Line, one of the world's leading ferry operators. As well as the Wales-Ireland route which forms the subject of this book, Stena also serve Holland, Scandinavia and, with a large fleet of freight vessels, ports all over the world.

In the pages that follow you will discover more about the history of the Fishguard-Rosslare route and the construction and development of the ports themselves. The train operations from Paddington and Dublin, so crucial to this story, are also described.

Finally, I wish to thank everyone who has helped with the creation of this book – your assistance has been invaluable, and a special note of gratitude must go to Eamonn Hewitt for so much guidance and encouragement.

Miles Cowsill
Ramsey, Isle of Man
June 2006

PREFACE

As Route Director of the Fishguard to Rosslare route it is my pleasant task to welcome you to a very special Centenary Book celebrating 100 years of the route. The book represents a faithful history of the route since its inception in 1906 and maps out the progression, latterly under Stena Line's stewardship, made since the early days of construction of Fishguard by the Great Western Railway. The fact that the route has always been a progressive one is well illustrated by the fact that in 1907 the GWR ran a day trip from Paddington to Killarney!

Ship names such as the ***St. Patrick***, ***St. David***, ***St. George*** and ***St. Andrew*** will evoke strong memories and emotions for many, not least on account of the bonding of two countries, Wales and Ireland, separated by only 54 miles of water. Fishguard has always been strategically well placed as a gateway to South Wales, the Midlands and the South East whilst Rosslare lies just 100 miles from Ireland's two main cities, Dublin and Cork. The road network on both sides of the Irish Sea continues to improve and thankfully the route continues to flourish.

Stena Line entered the Irish Sea in 1990 and is justifiably proud and privileged to play an ongoing part in the development of a very special route. To everyone ashore and afloat who has played such an important part in the history of the route - we thank you and salute you.

Vic Goodwin

Vic Goodwin
Route Director
Stena Line - Irish Sea

The **Stena Europe** *makes a fine view captured at night at Rosslare pending her 21.15 departure to Fishguard. (Gordon Hislip)*

StenaEXPRESS
stenaline.com

An outstanding view of the **Stena Lynx III** *and the* **Stena Europe** *off the port of Rosslare in August 2004. (Gordon Hislip)*

FOREWORD

For Stena Line and its association with this route and the British and Irish ferry industry, the publication of this book marks a special landmark. The Fishguard-Rosslare route opened as a vital link between Wales and Ireland in 1906 and it still remains an integral part of the transport system today, especially since both the UK and Ireland joined the European Union.

The route has played its role in two World Wars with its ships and crews from both sides of the St. George's Channel.

Today the ferry service is very different from when the route was established with four vessels, with only two employed on the service whilst the other two were used in reserve, a luxury unaffordable today and not required for that matter. Today the *Stena Europe* maintains the operation of conveying passengers and their cars all year round together with a most vital role for export and import trade by freight operators. In summer the combination of the *Stena Europe* and our fast ferry, the *Stena Express*, allows us to provide an unmatched capacity, frequency and speed in a most efficient manner.

Dan Sten Olsson

This publication is meant to stand as a fitting tribute to the ships, crews and shore staff, who have served with the GWR, British Rail, Sealink and Stena Line over the last 100 years. We are truly indebted for your work and efforts which have contributed to the success and development of this important route on the Irish Sea.

Many thanks to those involved with this publication, especially Miles Cowsill, who has researched the history of the route and pulled the title together.

I hope you will enjoy this anniversary book which illustrates how this route, by improvements and adaptability to change, has contributed to the development of trade and transport to the benefit of Wales and Ireland over the years.

Dan Sten Olsson
Chairman of Stena Line / CEO of Stena AB Group

The **Stena Europe** *arriving at Rosslare during her first season on the route in March 2002. (Gordon Hislip)*

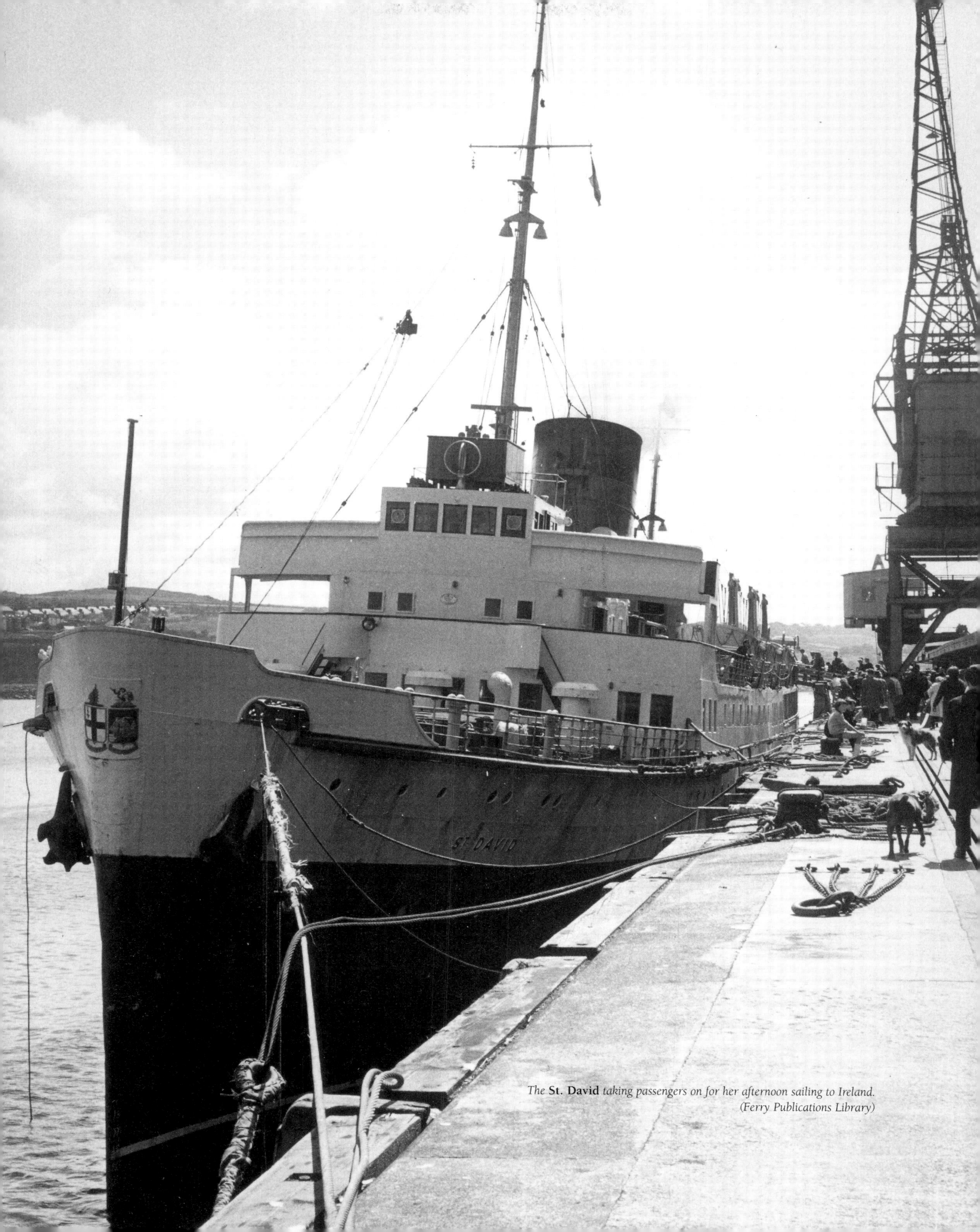

The **St. David** *taking passengers on for her afternoon sailing to Ireland.*
(Ferry Publications Library)

An early view of the port of Fishguard with one of the 'Saint' class vessels at the berth pending her afternoon sailing to Rosslare. Behind this vessel can be seen the tender **Sir Francis Drake** *and one of the ships of the City of Cork Steam Packet Company. (National Museums & Galleries of Wales)*

CHAPTER ONE

THE BUILDING OF FISHGUARD HARBOUR

by Martin Lewis

From a point early in his career, it was the declared ambition of Isambard Kingdom Brunel to create a "public highway" from London to New York - all this at a time when railway transport was in its infancy, and maritime travel was totally dependent on sail power. With the construction of the railway line from Paddington to Bristol, and the successful construction of his vessel, the *Great Western*, the first vessel to be powered by steam and the first to be constructed with a non-timber hull, he had achieved his ambition at an early age.

Brunel, however, was not one to rest on his laurels. We have to remember that, in the middle of the nineteenth century, the country was experiencing the Industrial Revolution. The attendant railway "mania" simply facilitated this. Apart from his far reaching projects involving the extension of the broad gauge, the building of bridges, ships, mobile hospitals (for the Crimean War) etc, he believed that developing trade with Ireland was of paramount importance for both countries. His broad gauge railway spread westwards reaching Haverfordwest in 1854. Whilst at one time he thought of building a railway across North Pembrokeshire to a proposed jetty at Goodic, it was an Act of Parliament in 1848 which authorised the development to be carried out at Abermawr - a point further along the coast about 8 miles west of Fishguard. Indeed, construction work was started there shortly afterwards. However, as a result of the potato famine, the economic situation in Ireland at this time was dire, and plans for the development were shelved.

Tragically, Brunel died in 1859, shortly after he had inspected his last creation, the Royal Saltash Bridge over the River Tamar. His genius and creativity were now lost to the Great Western Railway. His legacy however was very much appreciated by the travelling public, and many of his ambitions remained in the minds of the directors of the GWR including that of creating a harbour at 'Goodic' - a point on the North Pembrokeshire coast which was as near as was practical (55 miles) to the Irish coast and, most importantly, sheltered from the prevailing westerly winds.

This interesting postcard from the turn of the 19th century shows Goodwick prior to the development of the port. (Martin Lewis collection)

To build a harbour at 'Goodic', some difficult problems would have to be overcome. It would be necessary (a) to raise the necessary capital to undertake the work, (b) to blast away the rock face and create a large platform for the railway network and quayside, (c) to create protection from the hostile northerly and easterly winds which had wrecked so many vessels in previous centuries, (d) to provide sufficient housing for railway and quayside workers, (e) to deal with the problem of the fishermen's quay, and (f) to make ancillary provision e.g.for engineering and maintenance workshops, a power house, cattle lairage, hotel accommodation, dredging facilities etc. The Fishguard Bay Railway and Pier Act of 1893 authorised the building of a jetty and a short length of railway line to connect with the North Pembrokeshire & Fishguard Railway (NP&FR) at Goodwick station.

An independent line, the Maenclochog Railway, had been built to transport minerals from Rosebush to the main line at Narberth Road (Clynderwen). An Act of Parliament dated 1878 authorised the extension of the line, now renamed the Rosebush and Fishguard Railway (later the NP&FR) to Goodwick Station, but no more than a mile of track had been laid towards Fishguard when problems were encountered. In 1892, a Birmingham solicitor, Joseph Rowlands along with a fellow townsman named Cartland, acquired a controlling interest in the NP&FR and at the same time purchased the Rosslare Harbour works. Following this purchase, progress was rapid. It was a speculative venture which Rowlands subsequently attempted to sell to the GWR. After years of resistance, purchase by the GWR finally came about in 1898, prompted partly out of its policy for general advancement of its network but more out of a fear that the asset would be sold to its sworn enemy - the London and North Western Railway. Eventually, the GWR took control of the line, and on 1st July, one year later, the first steam train pulled into Goodwick station drawn by the 0-4-0 saddle tank. The railhead, however, still stopped about one mile short of the harbour facility as we know it today.

The Clarbeston Road to Letterston Junction rail link was required to pass through the Treffgarne Gorge , pictured here, a venture which almost drove the constructors to bankruptcy. (Martin Lewis collection)

GWR Directors were frequent visitors to the area, and stayed at the Wyncliffe Hotel which they later acquired. Subsequently, following major additions and adaptations, it became the

The Hotel Wyncliffe on the right (above) was formerly the home of the Rogers family - merchant adventurers from Devon. It was acquired by the GWR and subsequently developed as the Fishguard Bay Hotel - see page 91. (Martin Lewis collection)

The Harbour took longer to build than originally anticipated; in all 100 contracting staff and 400 GWR men were engaged in its construction. This view shows some of the staff involved with this impressive project. (Martin Lewis collection)

Fishguard Bay Hotel.

The journey from Paddington to Clynderwen was pleasant enough, but at the end of a long journey they soon grew tired of the slow train which drew them through the scenic beauty of the Preseli Hills, with its infinity of gradients and bends. It was easy enough to take the decision that a faster route should be created, and this, through an Act of Parliament of August 1898, led to the building of the link line from Clarbeston Road to Letterston Junction. It was specified that this should have no sharp bends and contain no steep gradients. Grave difficulties were encountered at Treffgarne Gorge which almost bankrupted the constructors, and it became necessary for them to go back to the GWR to ask for additional funds to complete the work. The link however was opened one day before the harbour facility at Fishguard was opened.

Having now acquired the NP&FR, the Rosslare Harbour works and the Fishguard Bay Railway and Pier Company formed in 1893, the GWR teamed up with the Great Southern & Western Company of Ireland to form the Fishguard & Rosslare Railways and Harbours Company. Between them they provided

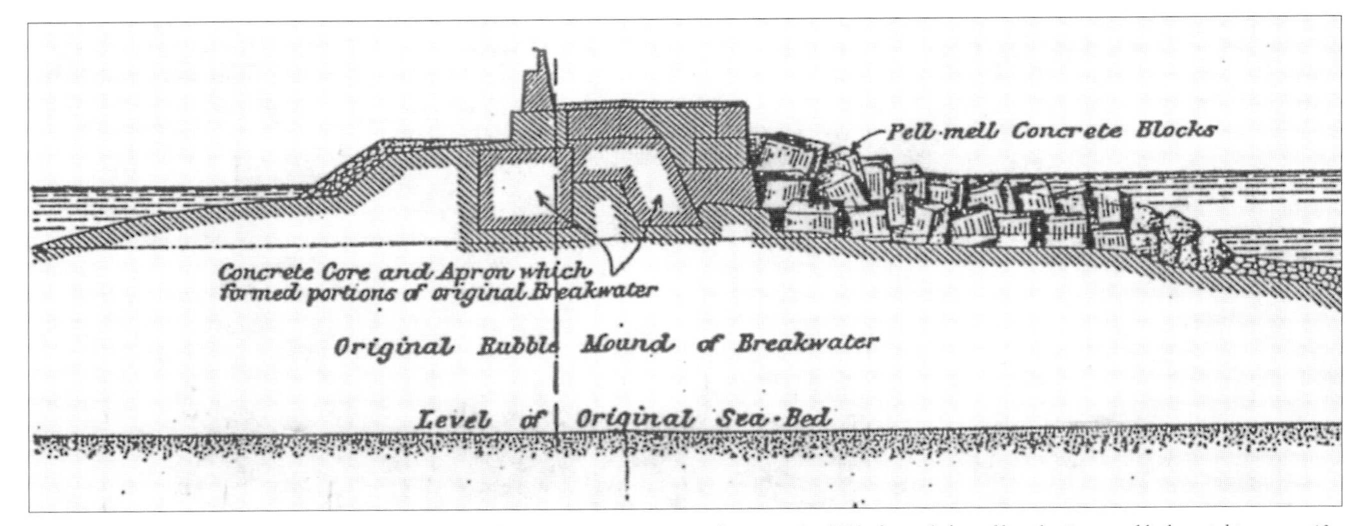

The drawing above shows a cross-section of the north breakwater requiring 650 tons of stone and rubbble for each foot of length. Concrete blocks weighing some 40 tons each were placed on the north side to counter the ravages of the sea and the north winds.

Harbour village, Goodwick. The housing stock in Fishguard and Goodwick was not adequate to meet the requirements when GWR transferred its activities from Neyland to Fishguard. This view shows houses under construction, which were built at a cost of up to £175 each. (Martin Lewis collection)

or guaranteed the capital necessary for the building and development of facilities on both sides of the channel. Much of the capital was also raised by the issue of shares.

In order to create the harbour at Fishguard, it was necessary to establish a platform with an area of 27 acres at the foot of a near vertical cliff almost 200 feet high in places. There were very few footholds on the cliff face such that men had to be lowered down by rope from the top of the cliff in order to enable them to establish a working platform. Once this had been completed, the work then became very much easier. Pneumatic drills were used to cut holes, 4 feet wide by 6 feet high to a depth of up to 50 feet into the rock face. Further cross-heads up to 50 feet wide were then cut to form a T-shape. The whole cavity was then packed and sealed with up to 10 tons of high explosive. As much as 100,000 tons of rock might be loosened whenever the explosive was fired. Nearly 2.5 million tons of rock were eventually removed from the rock face in this way. Much of this was used to build the harbour platform, and for general railway ballast. It is estimated that about 150 men were employed on handling the rocks and stones.

Many ships had been driven ashore during the 18th and 19th centuries - onto the rocks or the beach at Goodwick. The GWR authorities realised that it would be difficult to use the harbour when northerly winds were blowing, and that some protection from these winds was imperative. Construction of the north breakwater was commenced immediately. Rock slabs exceeding three tons in weight were placed on the more exposed north side of the breakwater whilst those of lesser size (but weighing more than one hundred-weight) were placed on the more sheltered south side. The breakwater was built in 70 feet of water and was 300 feet wide at its base, tapering to 70 feet at its upper side which stood twenty feet above the mean sea level. It is estimated that 650 tons of rock were required for each one foot length of the original 2,000 foot long breakwater. This was later extended by a further 900 feet. Substantial quantities of concrete were also used to strengthen the foundations. In addition to this, pell-mell block work (concrete blocks weighing up to 40 tons each) was carefully placed on the northerly side by the massive crane *Titan*.

In 1900, Fishguard and Goodwick were no more than villages, and housing would be inadequate for the large influx of personnel expected from New Milford, Neyland. Indeed, the staff at New Milford had been advised to be ready to move to the new harbour by 1902. The GWR had already purchased land above the rock face overlooking the Harbour. Over the next five years, more than a hundred houses were built at what we now know as Harbour Village. Some of these were ready for occupation by 1905. These were two-and three-bedroomed houses with the most expensive ones costing £175 to build. They were modern houses, among the very few in the country benefiting, at that time, from an electrical power supply provided from the Power House at the Harbour. A direct path was made down the steep slope separating the Village and the Harbour so as to allow residents/workers easy and rapid access to their workplace. This housing provision however proved to be inadequate, and the GWR built a further 50 houses in close proximity to its locomotive depot at Goodwick, enabling the GWR to call on its servants at short notice.

A large proportion of the male residents at Goodwick were, at this time, engaged in the fishing industry. To this end, they

Cattle lairages at Fishguard Harbour. Cattle disembarked at a level below that of the passengers and were walked along a ledge built into the quay wall and then used their own subway to gain access to the lairages. (Martin Lewis collection)

had established for themselves a jetty at the waterside below the Wyncliffe Hotel. They were adamant that they were not going to abandon this facility, and they held out for some time. The officers of the GWR, however, ultimately prevailed on them to leave their location on condition that the company would build for them a new and better facility. This was eventually constructed near the Goodwick end of the Marsh Sidings. Although this was of a more substantial nature, the depth of water afforded was not always adequate for those wishing to put to sea.

By July of 1906, a quay wall some 1,120 feet long had been completed as had the harbour rail network. There was thus sufficient quay space to accommodate vessels for the Rosslare, Waterford and Cork services at the same time. Two railway platforms, each 879 feet long, were in place. These were numbered from No.1 nearest the cliff face to No.4 nearest the quay wall. Platforms 1 and 2 were those used for the crack express boat trains, and No.3 would be used exceptionally for local passenger trains. Platform No.4 was used for goods in transit and refuelling purposes only. The station canopy covered all the platforms. The facility included two subways - one for passengers and the second for cattle. The cattle lairage had been erected although it had not been roofed over.

In addition to this, a mobile traverser, which was normally stowed beneath the platforms, could be brought into service to 'bridge' the gap between platforms 2 and 3. This obviated the need for passengers to use the subway when moving from the quay wall to catch the express trains.

By the middle of August of the same year, a great deal of work remained to be done, and this went on for many years afterwards. The Wyncliffe Hotel was being converted into what we now know as the Fishguard Bay Hotel. Immediately

The staff at Fishguard Harbour went on strike for more pay in 1911: the GWR were eager to settle rather than run the risk of disrupting Cunard Line traffic. Shortly after settlement there was a call for a national strike which staff at Fishguard joined. The Army were sent in during this industrial unrest and are pictured here billeted in the Marsh Sidings. (Martin Lewis collection)

below the Hotel, a space previously occupied by contractors' plant and machinery was being developed as the Marsh Sidings - railway sidings providing sufficient space for up to 200 railway wagons.

Most importantly however, three brand new vessels, named after the patron saints, were heading for Fishguard, and these were to be used on the Rosslare service. The *St. George*, built by Cammel Lairds, and the *St. Patrick* built by John Brown of Clydebank, both arrived on 21st August 1906. The *St. David*, also built by John Brown, arrived three days later. All vessels were registered in the name of the Fishguard & Rosslare Railways and Harbours Company (and not the GWR). Although the harbour was far from a state of completion, it was nonetheless opened, without due ceremony, on 30th August of the same year.

This view shows one of the working cranes at Fishguard Harbour about a year after the port had opened. The buildings are taking shape on the quay wall and work still continues on the Atlantic Wharf (at the near end of the breakwater). Much work still remains to be done on the 2,000 ft. breakwater. (Martin Lewis collection)

The new ships, the Saints, were pressed into service immediately. They had been built specially for the Fishguard-Rosslare run and were considered to be 'state of the art' vessels of their time. They were ships of nearly two-and-a-half thousand tons displacement, each with two funnels painted red and topped with a band of black. (Was this an effort to emulate the colours of the Cunard liners?) They were powered by steam turbines driving a triple-screw propeller arrangement. They were capable of 22.5 knots (equivalent to nearly 26 mph). This was almost as fast as the 'Blue Riband' holder across the Atlantic Ocean, and meant that the Irish Channel could be crossed in less than three hours. There were two sailings in each direction each day, each vessel being put into service in turn.

This view shows the Fishermens' Quay which replaced the original Fishguard Harbour in 1905 prior to the completion of the outer breakwater. Visible in the bay are the Brixham trawlers which were frequent visitors to the Pembrokeshire coast at the turn of the century. (Martin Lewis collection)

At the time when the ferry services were transferred from Neyland to Fishguard, the GWR felt that services to Rosslare - run by the GWR, and those to Cork - run by the City of Cork Steam Packet Company, would suffice the needs of the travelling public. The Irish authorities however were unhappy about this, and insisted that a clause be included in the Act of Incorporation (of the F&RRH Co.) requiring that 'the service to Waterford be maintained to at least the level appertaining at the time of the Act.'

The **Pembroke**, *originally a paddle steamer, was transferred from Neyland to Fishguard. She along with the* **Great Southern** *and* **Great Western** *provided the service to Waterford. She is seen here arriving at Fishguard. (Martin Lewis collection)*

The vessels, the *Great Southern*, the *Great Western* and a converted paddle steamer the s.s. *Pembroke* were thus brought to Fishguard to provide this service. These ships were necessarily a little smaller than the Saints because they were required to travel up the river to Waterford - a service which was provided on a daily basis. Publicity ensured that the public were encouraged to use the Rosslare route and, for a long time, passenger numbers to Waterford were closely scrutinised. Despite this, the service continued into the 1960's.

The service to Cork was the only one which was not organised and provided by the Great Western Railway. The ships initially used on this run were the *Inniscarra* and the *Innisfallen*. (Three versions of the *Innisfallen* were employed between 1906 and the 1960s), Indeed, the very first vessel to use the harbour facility was the *Inniscarra* (see page 114). Cork was a distance of 192 miles from Fishguard. The vessels from Cork would undertake the outward journey on Mondays, Wednesdays and Fridays making the return journey on Tuesdays, Thursdays and Saturdays. The Sabbath day was considered to be a day of rest when the vessels remained in their home port.

Two vessels would have been perfectly adequate to provide the service to Rosslare. It is intriguing therefore why the fourth vessel - the *St. Andrew* - was added to this complement. She did not arrive at the Harbour until two years or so after the opening in August 1906. If it could be considered that there was one vessel surplus to requirements before the arrival of the *St. Andrew*, it could certainly be said to be true afterwards. This was confirmed when the *St. George* was sold to a Canadian shipping line c.1911. Shortly after this, she served as a hospital ship in the First World War. This state of play remained, viz. three Patron Saints providing the service to Rosslare, a daily service to Waterford, with the City of Cork Steam Packet Company providing the service to Cork on alternate days. Much greater excitement was to follow exactly three years after the initial opening of the Harbour when the Cunard Liners began to call on their return journey from the United States of America.

To promote the new ferry service and also the connection with Cunard's operations from America, the GWR painted a series of buses in London. (Martin Lewis collection)

A relatively modern view of the current infrastructure at Fishguard. Today the port is used regularly by the conventional passenger ferry with two sailings a day, which are supplemented during the peak period by a fast ferry operation. This view, taken in 1990, shows the **Felicity** *at the linkspan which was built in 1972. (FotoFlite)*

GREAT WEST

MAURETANIA

G.W.R. T
FETCH
PASSE
Baggage

PLYMOUTH

MEETING T

RN RAILWAY

NDERS
CARRY
NGERS
& Mails

FISHGUARD

E BIG SHIPS

CHAPTER TWO

THE MAURETANIA AT FISHGUARD

by Miles Cowsill

In 1897 the Norddeutscher Lloyd ship *Kaiser Wilhelm der Grosse* took the Blue Riband from Cunard's *Campania* and *Lucania*. Thereafter German ships held the trophy without challenge. It was not until 1902 that negotiations began between the Government and Cunard with a view to building two superliners, the *Lusitania* and *Mauretania*, which would be capable of winning back and holding the Blue Riband for Britain. By 1903 an agreement had been reached whereby the Government would lend £2,600,000 to Cunard to build two ships capable of 24 to 25 knots. In addition they agreed to make an annual payment to Cunard on the condition that the two ships were capable of being armed and that the Government would have a claim on their services in times of national emergency.

The *Mauretania* was launched by the Duchess of Roxburgh. She was a quadruple-screw ship driven by direct-drive steam turbines. Although the propulsion machinery was identical to that of the *Lusitania* two modifications gave the *Mauretania* a slight edge over her sister. The diameter of the propeller blades was slightly larger and the turbines were fitted with more rows of blades.

The *Mauretania* made her maiden voyage from Liverpool on 16th November 1907. Severe storms hampered the first voyage but the ship still arrived in New York in good time on 22nd November. By April of the next year the *Mauretania* had captured both eastbound and westbound records and retained the Blue Riband for 20 years, until July 1929.

By 1909 the public was looking for faster crossings and, once at their destination, a speedy land journey. As a result it was inevitable that a port closer to London than Liverpool was required, and soon Fishguard was being developed as a port of call for Atlantic liners. The *Mauretania* was the first Cunard liner to use this port, on 30th August 1909.

The reputation of the ship attracted several prominent passengers. On a voyage during December 1910 Prince Albert and Prince Radziwell were amongst the passengers, along with Mr. Carlisle, the Managing Director of Harland & Wolff. In June 1911 the ship brought thousands of visitors to Britain for the Coronation of King George V.

When Britain declared war on Germany, on 4th August 1914, the ship was on her way to New York. At the last minute she was diverted to Halifax, Nova Scotia and the Admiralty sent out an order requisitioning the ship as an armed merchant cruiser, as soon as she returned to Liverpool. On 11th August, however, the *Mauretania* and the *Lusitania* were released from Government duties.

The reduced demand for trans-Atlantic passages meant that the ship was laid up at Liverpool on 26th August. After the loss of the *Lusitania* in May 1915 the *Mauretania* was required to return to service. Before she did, however, the Admiralty requisitioned the ship to transport troops during the Gallipoli

The **Mauretania** *was launched in 1906 by the Duchess of Roxburgh. She made her maiden voyage from Liverpool on 16th November 1907. (Martin Lewis collection)*

This wonderful detailed view shows the **Mauretania** *during her first visit to Fishguard with the tender drawing alongside her to disembark passengers. (National Museums & Galleries of Wales)*

The **Mauretania** *dressed overall is seen here again on her first visit to Fishguard. (National Museums & Galleries of Wales)*

campaign, later in May. During this period the ship made several voyages to Mudros Bay on the island of Lemnos, the Allied base for operations in the area. On one of these voyages the *Mauretania* was attacked by a submarine but managed to avoid the torpedo, largely due to the ship's high speed. At the end of August she returned to Liverpool and was fitted out as a hospital ship. She then left Liverpool on 21st October to assist with the evacuation of the wounded from Gallipoli. The *Mauretania* made several further voyages as a hospital ship and completed her last of these on 25th January 1916.

This, however, was not the end of the ship's war service. On 29th September she was requisitioned again to carry Canadian troops. In October-November 1916 she made two voyages from Liverpool to Halifax carrying Canadian troops bound for France. After this she was laid up on the Clyde until 1918. In March 1918 she was again used as a troopship carrying over 30,000 American troops before the Armistice in November. After the end of the War the ship was used in the repatriation of American and Canadian troops. From 12th December it was decided that the *Mauretania* would now sail from Southampton and call at Cherbourg on her way to New York. She made her final trooping voyage on 28th June 1919 and was then refitted at Southampton.

On 21st September 1919 she sailed from Southampton on her first commercial voyage since The Great War had begun. An overhaul, planned for 1920, was delayed as the demand for passenger services to Europe from America was so great. Whilst docked at Southampton, on 22nd July 1921, a fire broke out on board. The fire spread quickly and required the efforts of both the fire brigade and crew to extinguish it. The damage caused was confined to the First Class cabin area. It was decided to send the ship back to the builder's yard for an overhaul and the opportunity would be taken to convert from coal to oil-burning. By March 1922 the *Mauretania* had resumed her usual service.

On 25th July the ship broke her pre-war Atlantic speed record, with an average speed of above 26 knots. In January 1923 she was chartered by an American travel company and made a special Mediterranean cruise.

In 1924 the Cowes Harbour Commission complained about the *Mauretania's* speed as she left the Solent. The heavy wash

created had flooded Cowes main street and caused considerable disruption. The Government decided that the pilot was to blame. A refit in 1928 saw the ship's furniture and decor modernized. New ships built for the Norddeutscher Lloyd Line, however, were now posing a threat to the *Mauretania's* domination of the Atlantic. The ships *Europa* and *Bremen* were launched in August 1928. The *Bremen* soon broke the Atlantic speed record but the margin of time was quite small.

On 27th November 1929 the *Mauretania* collided with a train ferry near Robbins Reef, after leaving New York. Luckily no one was injured but the ship's bows were damaged. The hole in the bows, however, was repaired within 24 hours. After a winter overhaul she returned to service in February 1930 and during the following years concentrated mainly on cruising.The *Mauretania* made her final passenger sailing from Southampton on 30th June 1934, the day Cunard and White Star Lines merged. After two cruises to the West Indies she returned to Southampton on 2nd October. The completion of the *Queen Mary* and the merger with White Star meant that the fleet had to be reduced.

The *Mauretania* was now outdated and was soon laid up at Southampton. The ship was purchased on 3rd April 1935 by Metal Industries Ltd. of Glasgow for scrap. All the fixtures and fittings were auctioned on 14th May at Southampton Docks. On 1st July the ship left for the Tyne. On 3th July she reached the Firth of Forth and was then moved to Rosyth for dismantling.

Fact File - Mauretania

- Gross Tonnage - 31,938 tons
- Dimensions - 232.31 x 26.82m (762.2 x 88.0ft)
- Propulsion - Quadruple-screw
- Engines - Steam turbines by Wallsend Slipway Co. Ltd.
- Service speed - 25 knots
- Builder - Swan, Hunter & Wigham Richardson, Wallsend-on-Tyne
- Launch date - 20th September 1906
- Passenger accommodation - 563 1st class, 464 2nd class, 1,138 3rd class

FISHGUARD: THE GATEWAY TO BRITAIN

Above: *A passenger tender leaves the* **Mauretania** *and heads for the quay of Fishguard Harbour to enable passengers to embark on the train to Paddington. (National Museums & Galleries of Wales)*

Top right: *Such was the interest in the arrival of the* **Mauretania** *at Fishguard that many local people in Pembrokeshire came to the port to see this event. This postcard shows crowds on the hill at Goodwick overlooking the Harbour with the* **Mauretania** *in the bay between the still-to-be completed breakwater and the promontory of Dinas Head. (Martin Lewis collection)*

Middle right: *This view shows mail being loaded onto one of the tenders from the* **Mauretania**. *(National Museums & Galleries of Wales)*

Right:: *This view shows some of the first passengers to disembark the Cunard liner, the* **Mauretania**, *waiting to board the train to Paddington. (National Museums & Galleries of Wales)*

MAURETANIA

The **Mauretania** *waits to pull away from Fishguard Bay following her first visit to Fishguard. (National Museums & Galleries of Wales)*

CHAPTER THREE

ROSSLARE - A PORT IS CROWNED

by John Maddock

The opening of the Rosslare-Fishguard service in 1906 marked the beginning of an historic new chapter in the development of South East Ireland and in particular the Port of Rosslare Harbour and its immediate environs.A century later, the port is thriving with regular services to Britain and Continental Europe but the outstanding constant for the 100 years has been the Rosslare-Fishguard link.

Overlooking the busy port is what began as the village of Rosslare Harbour in the early 1900s and has since become an expanded community with a population of a few thousand.More than half a century before the start of the service from Rosslare Harbour to Fishguard, commercial interests on both sides of St George's Channel had yearned for the day when the 54-mile divide of sea would have a regular steamer service. The development of steamships and railways whetted ambitions and the potential benefits of such a link were obvious.If a regular shipping service could be opened on the route with connecting railway links on both sides of the Channel, greater prosperity would result.Shipowners and railway companies envisaged a good future for their operations while the shipping industry in general was calling for a new "port of refuge" on Ireland's busy South East coast. The ancient Port of Wexford, on the estuary of the River Slaney and some 10 miles to the north-west of the present port of Rosslare Harbour, had handled most of the shipping commerce of the area for centuries. It had regular cross-channel sea links and was home to a fine fleet of its own ships, particularly in the days of sail, but Wexford port had its limitations. The broad harbour leading to the quays at Wexford was not deep enough to cater for the ever-increasing size of ships. At the mouth of the harbour was Wexford Bar, made up

An early view of Rosslare Harbour with a cargo sailing ship unloading her timber at the port taken in the late 1870s. (John Maddock collection)

An early view of Rosslare Harbour taken in the late 1800s. (John Maddock collection)

of treacherous and shifting sandbanks which claimed many vessels, including the brand new steamer *Slaney* which was lost as she tried to enter Wexford in January 1885. The *Slaney* had been completed just two months earlier for the Wexford-Liverpool route to carry passengers and cargo. Interested groups in Ireland and Britain were campaigning as early as the 1830s for new harbours in Co. Wexford and Pembrokeshire to serve a modern steamer service with railway connections.On the Irish side, interests in the Port of Wexford would have preferred if their port had been chosen as the terminal but locations around the shores of Rosslare Bay - or Greenore Bay or the South Bay as it was variously known - and further southwards along the Co. Wexford coast were being mooted.The townland of Ballygeary, bordering on Greenore Bay and now the location of Rosslare Harbour, was always a front runner. Strongly in its favour was the shelter it afforded for vessels from the prevailing south-westerly winds.In 1846, legislation was enacted in the London Parliament for the laying of a railway from Dublin, Wicklow and Waterford to "a pier in the sea or on the shore of Greenore Bay near the Town and Port of Wexford".That legislation - the Waterford, Wexford, Wicklow and Dublin Railway Act - was a major breakthough but factors were to emerge which halted its intentions. Within months of its enactment, the Great Famine broke out in Ireland as the potato crop, the staple diet of the masses, developed blight and failed nationally.The crop again failed in "Black '47" and the following years. A million Irish people died in those terrible years and another million emigrated, mostly to Britain and the United States. The economy of Ireland was in ruins and the development of new harbours and shipping links in the South East slipped far down the list of priorities, even though Co. Wexford escaped the worst ravages of the Famine. It took the country decades to recover from the effects of the horrors of the late 1840s. It was not until 1863 that there was further legislation providing for the construction of railways in South East Ireland and "a pier and harbour to be situate in Greenore Bay at the termination of the railway or branch railway in the townland of Ballygeary." There was to be still further delay until 1873 when Rosslare Harbour Commissioners acquired a portion of land to build a new harbour but the planned project was beset with funding difficulties.Construction work on a new pier proceeded during the 1870s. By 1877 the pier was not completed but it was being used by some ships and local fishing vessels. The opening of the railway from Wexford to Kilrane - just short of Rosslare Harbour in June 1882 was a further advance in the port's development. A new port had opened and was trading, if only on a limited basis.The regular Wexford-Liverpool steamer *Montague* was held up for two days in February 1883 because she could not cross Wexford Bar in adverse weather. In an unscheduled move, the *Montague* disembarked her passengers at the unfinished pier at Rosslare Harbour. The occasion was not marked by fanfare but it was historic and it was probably the first occasion on which

This view shows the **St. David** *(I) at Rosslare Harbour shortly after the opening of the Fishguard-Rosslare service. (John Maddock collection)*

passengers were landed at the port.Financial problems seriously slowed development to such a pitch that in 1885 a deputation of nearly 20 Irish MPs met the Secretary of the British Treasury in London to press for a grant of £40,000 to complete the port. In the late 1880s, the regular Wexford-Bristol steamer *Briton* docked at Rosslare Harbour on several occasions to load livestock for the British market.During the next decade, the still unfinished port was used by a number of ships but the then 60-year-old dream of a regular cross-channel steamer link out of Rosslare remained unfulfilled until 1896. Even then, the service that did open was not railway-linked and was not to a short-sea destination in Pembrokeshire.Legislation of the 1890s allowed for the development of Fishguard Harbour and the completion of the long-awaited plans for Rosslare Harbour. Under legislation in 1894, the old Waterford and Wexford Railway Co. and Rosslare Harbour Commissioners were vested in Fishguard & Rosslare Railways and Harbours Co. The Great Western Railway in Britain and Great Southern and Western Railways in Ireland became partners in the new venture, but clearly it was going to be some years before the actual Rosslare-Fishguard service could begin. As an interim measure, a shipping service from Rosslare to Bristol and Liverpool opened on 26th August 1896.The route was served by the 612-ton chartered steamer *Voltaic* which on her first trip from Rosslare to Bristol carried 11 passengers, 30 pigs and 78 sheep. The little *Voltaic* maintained the service for four years until April 1900. She encountered severe competition from rival vessels running from Wexford to Bristol and Liverpool. Her rivals recognised the advantages of Rosslare port and sometimes used it when Wexford was inaccessible in poor weather. The decades of disappointment for Rosslare Harbour, however, were nearing an end. As the new century dawned, extensive developments at both Rosslare and Fishguard were taking place in preparation for the grand opening of the new route in 1906.In the early 1900s, a new 1,550 foot long pier was built at Rosslare Harbour to provide berthage not only for new ships to serve the route to Fishguard but also general cargo vessels and fishing craft. The pier was along the same path as the old incomplete pier which had been in use since the 1870s.Three brand new mail steamers - the *St. Patrick*, *St. David* and *St. George* - were being built for the opening of the new route while a fourth, the *St. Andrew*, was to follow in 1908, and to complete the "dream" of 60 years earlier of having a fast rail-linked shipping service across St George's Channel, a railway was laid across a new viaduct from the pier to link Rosslare Harbour with Waterford and on to the South of Ireland generally. Along the east coast, the railway from Wexford and Dublin was extended to run along the new pier.The developments had a tremendous impact on the Rosslare Harbour locality which has always been very conscious of its maritime dependancy. Over the centuries, the population of the area had lived off the land and the sea. The general area has a long and illustrious maritime tradition.A coastguard station was

Early days at Ballygeary Pier, Rosslare Harbour in the 1880s. (John Maddock collection)

built at Rosslare Harbour in 1869 and the adjacent Lighthouse Dwellings - for off-duty lightkeepers from Tuskar Rock Lighthouse, seven miles offshore - were opened in 1887. A lifeboat station opened at Rosslare Harbour in 1896 although there had been another station at Rosslare Fort, a few miles to the north, for some decades earlier. In the 1920s, the station at the Fort closed and all operations were centred at Rosslare Harbour. There were just a few houses or shops adjacent to the Harbour at the turn of the century. The local centre of activity was the little village of Kilrane, a mile from the port.The five or six years up to 1906 saw significant construction work on the new pier and railways and those involved had to be accommodated temporarily in the neighbourhood, some of them in specially-built temporary dwellings.Simultaneously, accommodation had to be provided for the many workers who would be employed permanently at the port and on the railways. Forty-four new houses in four streets were built for the permanent railway and port employees. The "railway houses" still form a distinct area of Rosslare Harbour. A dormitory for overnighting train crews was built.Near the houses, the Railway Social Club was opened and a century later it is still flourishing as a social centre for the locality. Next door to "the club", Rosslare Harbour Co-operative Society Ltd began a retail business which was to last for more than 60 years.Welcoming delegates to a national conference of Co-operative Societies in Rosslare Harbour in September 1910, the then local president Thomas Ryan, with just a little exaggeration, said:"I remember the time not so long ago when there was not a house on the Hill of Ballygeary, much less a society. In 1902 there was not a stone house to be seen. There are very many changes since then."A new roadway - still known as De Lap's Hill after the engineer who was in charge of the works in the early 1900s - was built from the Harbour to the clifftop. Wexford County Council built a further roadway through the growing village allowing residential and business premises to be built beside it. Gradually, over the years, the community expanded.The port, the railways and the ships on the Rosslare-Fishguard service brought good employment. Down through the past century, many of the crews of the vessels on the route have been drawn from the Rosslare/Wexford area, as well as from the Fishguard district.The opening of the route paved the way for new bonds to be forged between the communities of Rosslare Harbour and Fishguard. Many families from the Rosslare area set up home in Fishguard, particularly during times of economic depression in Ireland and especially in the bleak 1950s.In Ireland's "Celtic Tiger" years of unprecedented economic growth since the late 1990s, that trend has been reversed on a much lesser scale, with some descendants of Co. Wexford families in Wales finding work in Ireland. So convenient is the Rosslare-Fishguard service that families with relatives in Rosslare Harbour and Fishguard can easily cross the Channel to visit and be home the same night. The withdrawal of the mailboats on the Rosslare-Fishguard

This view shows one of the first Fishguard vessels, around 1910, at Rosslare Harbour. (John Maddock collection)

service during the two World Wars had serious economic consequences for the local community in Rosslare Harbour, as well as Fishguard. When the route re-opened in 1946 after World War II there was a truly genuine welcome but trade for the service was worryingly slack during the 1950s.The advent of the car ferries in the mid-1960s brought an immense surge of activity to Rosslare Harbour and the community. New hotels and guesthouses sprang up. The opening of other shipping services from the port to Britain and Continental Europe added to the general air of prosperity. Until the 1960s, the port as it was built for the opening of the 1906 service remained largely unchanged. It catered for the Fishguard ships and several cargo vessels - bringing in coal, timber, phosphates and other commodities and taking out agricultural produce, dairy products and moss peat. Live cattle made up a major export for many years. Just as Rosslare Harbour's geographical position had made it so attractive to commercial interests for a cross-channel service in the 1800s, the port became the focus of attention for a service to Continental Europe in the late 1960s. A service from Rosslare to Le Havre opened in 1968 and, while it was discontinued in 1972, Irish Continental Line re-opened it in 1973.Irish Ferries - which in the late 1980s became part of the newly organised Irish Continental Line organisation - now runs from Rosslare to Cherbourg and Roscoff as well as Pembroke Dock.The expansion of port shipping resulted in the construction of a second pier in the 1970s. In 1980, the old B & I Line of Dublin (also later brought within the Irish Ferries group) opened a new ferry service between Rosslare and Pembroke Dock. With more and more ships of vastly increasing tonnage using the port, a further major harbour development began in 1991 to provide another wharf to the west of the port, deeper water for all berths and the reclamation from the sea of an extensive area to accommodate the ever-increasing volume of trucks.Pandoro, part of the P & O Group, opened a service from Rosslare to Cherbourg in 1993. The P & O pulled out of the route in late 2004 but the service has been continued by the Co. Wexford-owned Celtic Link Ferries. United European Car Carriers (UECC) has frequent shipments of new cars into Rosslare.Hotels, guesthouses and a variety of businesses have opened in Rosslare Harbour in recent years and there has been substantial residential development. Just as those who in the mid-1880s could scarcely have believed that a regular rail-linked steamer service would open in 1906, the developers of that year could never have envisaged that what they began would lead to the Rosslare Harbour of today.

This view taken in the early 1990s shows the **Prinsessan Desiree** *and the* **Stena Normandica** *at Rosslare Harbour. (Miles Cowsill)*

This view takes in the **Cambridge Ferry**, **St. Patrick II** *and the chartered vessel ro-ro vessel* **Oleander** *at the new linkspan. (John Maddock collection).*

The **St. Patrick** *(I) is seen here on trials prior to entry into service. Fishguard boasted a fleet of four vessels of which only two were regularly kept in service on the required schedules. (Miles Cowsill collection)*

CHAPTER FOUR

FISHGUARD-ROSSLARE 1906-2006

by Miles Cowsill

TWO PORTS ARE BORN

The port of Fishguard is located in northern Pembrokeshire and is sheltered to the west by Crincoed Point and to the north by Dinas Head. The port boasts of being the nearest mainland harbour to Southern Ireland at a distance of only 54 nautical miles. Haverfordwest, the County Town of Pembrokeshire, is about 16 miles south of the port and London lies some 263 miles to the east. In recent years the road communications have improved from the port to the M4 with the up-grading of the A40. Likewise in Ireland vast improvements have been undertaken to the road system; the capital can be reached in under three hours, and within the next couple of years the drive between Rosslare and Dublin should be under two hours.

Fishguard is a relatively new port compared with the other ferry ports around our coast. Prior to the advent of Fishguard, the Great Western Railway operated to Ireland from Neyland (New Milford) which is located some 8 miles south of Haverfordwest on the Cleddau estuary.

The Great Western Railway reached Neyland in August 1856 and arrangements were made with a London firm by the name of Ford & Jackson to run a service between Neyland and Waterford. In 1871 the GWR obtained permission from the Government to operate its own service. The next year the GWR took over Ford & Jackson's operations, which included four vessels, for £45,500.

By 1874 a total of seven steamers was stationed at New Milford, though not all of them were in use at the same time, to operate the Waterford service. The following year saw the GWR open their own Cork service from Pembrokeshire - the link was only to last a year. The route was taken over by the City of Cork Steam Packet Company Limited, following the GWR closing their service on 1st June 1876.

By 1895 proposals were put forward for a major modernisation programme at New Milford for the port and the ships. These proposals were only to be short-lived, as far as New

Passengers board the ferry at Fishguard. This picture is believed to originate from only weeks after the port opening. (Martin Lewis collection)

Above: *The* **St. David** *approaches the quay wall on one of her early sailings on the St. George's Channel. (Martin Lewis collection)*

Above left: *This early view shows the stokers on board one of the 'Saint' vessels at Fishguard taking a well-earned rest between sailings. (Martin Lewis collection)*

Above right: *Another early view at Fishguard Harbour with passengers boarding the lunchtime sailing to Rosslare. (Martin Lewis collection)*

The **St. Patrick** *arrives at Rosslare during her early career on the route. (NRM/ Science and Society Picture Library)*

A fine view of the **St. George** *arriving at Fishguard. Built on the Mersey, she arrived ten days after the port opened. (Martin Lewis collection)*

Milford was concerned, as the GWR were now considering a move to Fishguard and opening a new terminal at Rosslare in Ireland. The ships were however ordered, as planned, to replace the paddle steamers. The new steamers named *Great Western* and *Great Southern* entered service in 1902 from New Milford, prior to the opening of the port of Fishguard.

The construction of Fishguard Harbour was authorised by the Fishguard and Rosslare Railways and Harbours Act of 1899. During the next few years no expense was to be spared in making Fishguard the port for Irish traffic, with the possible advantage of being used also as a trans-Atlantic terminal.

To provide sufficient area for the harbour station and the quay, large quantities of rock had to be blasted out of the cliff face; a total of 27 acres of land was created by this work. To protect the quay, two breakwaters of 800 metres had to be built. For every foot of length required for each breakwater, it took some 650 tons of stone. In addition to the harbour works at Fishguard, a new railway had to be built from Clarbeston Road (east of Haverfordwest) to the new port. Both these aspects are covered in other chapters in this book.

On the other side of the St. George's Channel, the GSWR of Ireland had to construct a new railway of 37 miles from Waterford to the port of Rosslare. Meanwhile, tenders for the Rosslare pier extension were sought in 1901 and the contract was won by Charles Brand & Company of Glasgow; work on reconstructing the pier began in May 1902. A detailed account

This view shows the GWR vessel **St. David** *at anchor in the bay on stand-by service. (Martin Lewis collection)*

A fine view of the **St. David** *taken at Fishguard prior to the First World War. One of her sisters can be seen in the background at anchor in the bay. (National Museums & Galleries of Wales)*

This view shows the Marsh Sidings and one of the early 'Saints' in Fishguard Harbour. There was a considerable volume of goods traffic to and from Ireland via Fishguard Harbour. Hand-operated points from the down goods loop led to seven sidings with capacity for holding up to 200 wagons. (Martin Lewis collection)

of the development and construction of the port is covered in Chapter 3 and the building of the railway line between Dublin and Waterford, and later on to Rosslare is covered in Chapter 6.

In 1903 the keels of the *St. Patrick* and *St. David* were laid at John Brown's yard on the Clyde. Cammell Laird's yard at Birkenhead was given the contract to build the third vessel, the *St. George*. Each ship was to cost £110,000. The *St. George* (2,571 tons) was first to be completed and the 352 foot long vessel was launched into the Mersey on 13th January 1906. The *St. David* of 2,456 tons was launched into the Clyde on 25th January 1906 and a month later the *St. Patrick* entered the water. All three vessels were practically identical with two full length decks and were fine-looking vessels with black hulls with red boot topping, with the two colours separated by a thin white line. The ships were designed to operate as both day and night vessels and were able accommodate over 1,000 passengers (572 First Class and 438 Second Class). There were 47 cabins provided and additional sleeping areas were provided aft on the decks for Second Class travellers.

THE NEW LINK OPENS

The official opening of the Fishguard - Rosslare service was to take place on Friday 30th August 1906. The *St Patrick* under the command of Captain Bournand opened the service inward to Pembrokeshire with 112 passengers at 13.05, while the *St David* under the command of Captain Davies made the first official westbound voyage at 14.35 with 231 passengers.

It is interesting to note at this point that there was a time difference between Britain and Ireland. As there was a 25 minute difference between Irish and British time, this meant that on eastbound sailings the ships' clocks were advanced 25 minutes, while on westbound sailings they were put back 25 minutes. This situation was to prevail until the outbreak of the First World War.

From the outset of the service two sailings daily in each direction were offered between Fishguard and Rosslare. On 13th September, the *St George* entered service on the 14.35 sailing from Fishguard to Rosslare with a mere 65 passengers. Some two days earlier the *St David* carried over a thousand passengers on the link for the first time. By October the average passenger loadings on each sailing had reached around fifty. In addition to the passenger operations, a cargo service at 09.55 sailed from Rosslare and from Fishguard at 14.00, with either the *Mercury* or the *Pembroke*.

On the opening of Fishguard Harbour, the Waterford and Cork passenger services were transferred to North Pembrokeshire from Neyland. The Waterford passenger link was maintained by two ships, while the Cork route was left in the capable hands of the City of Cork Steam Packet Company.

Two years after the Fishguard opening, the original trio of vessels was joined by a fourth sister from John Brown. The new ship entered service on 18th May 1908 in dense fog, sailing first from Fishguard. The arrival of the new ship, the *St. Andrew*, allowed one ship to be laid up for refitting, while two ships maintained the route, with one ship on stand-by,. The luxury of two ships on stand-by would be uneconomical and unthinkable nowadays!

By December 1909 the service was carrying an average of around 9,000 passengers per month with four vessels, none of which appeared to have an intense working pattern on inspection of the ports' records. In December 1909, the *St George* undertook fourteen sailings, the *St. David* two sailings, *St. Patrick* twenty-four sailings and the *St. George* eleven sailings in

The drawing room of the **St. David** *(I) taken in 1926. (National Museums & Galleries of Wales)*

The smoking room of the **St. David** *(I) taken in 1926. (National Museums & Galleries of Wales)*

the month. By September 1911, the route passenger carryings had increased to around 13,500 per month.

During June 1913, the *St George* was sold to the Canadian Pacific Railway Company as part of a reorganisation of the Fishguard-Rosslare service, when it was decided to operate the route in future with three vessels. She made her last crossing on 1st March 1913, on the 14.35 sailing to Ireland. Following her crossing of the Atlantic, she was employed in the Bay of Fundy between St John and Digby. In 1917 she was requisitioned during the First World War, then later sold to the Great Eastern Railway in 1919. Ten years later the vessel was scrapped.

Prior to the outbreak of the First World War, the route was carrying something in region of 15,000 passengers a month. The GWR were unsuccessful in attracting trans-Atlantic liner trade following the historic visit of the *Mauretania* during August 1909. The GWR made every effort to attract Cunard to the port but, sadly for Pembrokeshire, the famous company was to be wooed by Southampton.

THE WAR YEARS

When Britain mobilised herself for war during August 1914, the immediate effect for Fishguard was the 'calling up' of three of the steamers for use as hospital ships, leaving only the older Waterford boats to cope with the Rosslare service. On 7th August the service was closed for two days following the outbreak of war; prior to this the *St Patrick*, the *Great Southern* and the *Waterford* had been employed in troop movements on the St George's Channel.

The *St. Andrew*, *St David* and *St. Patrick* were altered internally as hospital ships at the marine workshops at Fishguard, prior to their departure for war. By September 1914, the route was in the hands of the *Great Southern*, *Great Western* and the *Duke of Connacht*. By April 1915 day sailings had been suspended and the link was operated by three vessels and the cargo ship *Dewsbury*. In spite of the war in July 1915 some 10,000 passengers were carried. February 1916 saw a strike on the link for a month, with the service opening again on 29th February with the *Great Southern*.

Recovery from the First World War was to be slow as far as the Fishguard - Rosslare service was concerned. The uncertain political situation in Ireland was to have an adverse effect on the route, and it was not until 1st January 1920 that all the three 'Saints' returned to the Rosslare service. On the same day the train service to Paddington was returned to something like pre-war levels.

In October 1920 the service was closed owing to a coal strike; this was followed by labour troubles which suspended operations until 3rd January 1921. In June 1922 the service closed again due to troubles in Ireland and it was not until 17th September 1923 the service re-opened with the *St. Andrew* sailing light from Fishguard to take up the 02.50 sailing from Rosslare. Meanwhile the *Great Southern* opened the link again from Pembrokeshire on 17th September, and some eight days later the *St. David* had taken her place on the route.

The Directors of the company employed the *St. Andrew* on a special cruise from Fishguard to Douglas, Isle of Man in September 1923 and on 24th June 1924 the *St.David* sailed from Fishguard to Plymouth and on to Brest and St Nazaire in France.

During 1925 the *St. David* was re-engined, followed a year later by the *St. Patrick*. The early Fishguard 'Saint' class were replaced by the *St. Patrick* (II), built by Alexander Stephen & Sons, Glasgow in 1930; the new vessel was to make her maiden voyage between Weymouth and the Channel Islands, a role she

Following the outbreak of the First World War the **St. George** *was pressed into service as a hospital ship. (Martin Lewis collection)*

The **St. Andrew** *(II) in the Mersey undergoing sea trials prior to entering service at Fishguard. (Williamson Art Gallery & Museum)*

ST. PATRICK 1930-1941

Owner:	Fishguard & Rosslare Railways and Harbours Co.
Builder:	Alexander Stephen & Sons Ltd, Linthouse, Glasgow
Yard No:	525
Launched:	15th January 1930
Maiden Voyage:	18th April 1930
Gross Tonnage:	1,922
Speed:	18 knots

The *St. Patrick* was built for the Fishguard-Rosslare service and as a relief vessel for the Weymouth-Channel Islands operations of the Great Western Railway; she was the second ship to bear the name at the port of Fishguard. The handsome-looking vessel was launched by Mrs J Milne, wife of the GWR's General Manager on 15th January 1930 at the Scottish yard of Alexander Stephen & Sons Ltd. She made her maiden voyage to Jersey and Guernsey on 18th April and made her debut on the Irish Sea in early September.

For the next nine years the ship served at Fishguard all year round apart from July and August when she was transferred to Weymouth. The Fishguard-based vessel was to have a fairly uneventful career, apart from her third season on the English Channel. On Friday 5th August 1932 she hit the rocks off the Corbiere lighthouse during a foggy approach to Jersey from Weymouth. She was eventually towed off with little damage.

The *St. Patrick* left the Channel Islands for the last time on 2nd September 1939. Following the outbreak of the Second World War, she was painted in battleship grey for her operations on the Fishguard-Rosslare service. During August 1940 the *St. Patrick* was bombed twice whilst on passage between Wales and Ireland. The first time she zigzagged at full speed, avoiding the bombs. The second time a passenger and one of the crew were wounded by machine-gun fire.

During the early morning of 13th June 1941 the *St. Patrick*, inward bound to Wales from Ireland under the command of Captain J Faraday, was bombed again by a German plane. The attack took place just before dawn within 15 miles of the Welsh coast. Reports from the crew at the time of the attack recalll a dark shape suddenly diving out of the sky on the port quarter and attacking the vessel with its machine guns. Instantly there was a reply from the machine-gun crew on the aft deck of the *St. Patrick*. Before the other gunners could get into action the plane had swung round and with a dive from immediately above the ship, she released a stick of bombs which struck the ship between the bridge and funnel amidships. There was a tremendous explosion which shook the ship violently from stem to stern, followed by a huge sheet of flame which completely enveloped the vessel's superstructure.

The attack took place in a matter of seconds and the officers and crew were momentarily stunned by the suddenness of the catastrophe and the force of the explosion. Following the attack there was very little panic and the crew sprang to emergency stations. The explosion had literally broken the ship in half and the divided crew fore and aft were left to their own resources. The bow portion of the vessel started to sink immediately; some of the crew, resting at the time in their bunks, barely had time to scramble on deck to release the rafts, which they followed into the sea.

Meanwhile a stirring drama was enacted aft, where almost all the passengers were asleep in their cabins. Aroused by the attack and the general commotion, they were helped from their bunks and marshalled to the stairway by members of the crew who had rushed to their assistance. Some of the passengers had managed to grasp a few articles of clothing, but the majority were in night attire. The ship was in complete darkness, the difficulty of dealing with the terrified passengers can be scarcely imagined, much less described, yet thanks to the magnificent work of the stewards, stewardess and seamen they were conducted onto the upper deck. Some of the women became hysterical, but they were comforted by the wonderful courage of the Stewardess, Miss May Owen, who was almost superhuman in her efforts to get them on deck.

Owing to the heavy list to starboard and the rapid way in which the ship was sinking, it was impossible to release the lifeboats and only the emergency boat on the quarter deck was launched. Fortunately the seamen had cut adrift the floating seats and rafts, and it was to these that the passengers clung when they plunged into the cold and dark Irish Sea.

The members of the engine-room staff had a remarkable escape. Penned in the bowels of the ship they had to force their way through a terrific inrush of water before they could scramble up the emergency ladders and leap from the sinking steamer.

One of the last to leave the ship was Wireless Officer Campbell, who remained at his post sending out SOS messages until his cabin was flooded. The last woman to leave was Stewardess Owen, who had returned to a cabin to assist a child to the upper deck. On reaching the outer deck she dived into the sea only a moment or two before the *St. Patrick* made her way to the bottom.

Captain Faraday, it is believed, was killed whilst standing on the bridge with his youngest son, John Michael Faraday, who had accompanied his father on the voyage during his holiday leave. Frank Rowe, Chief Officer and the Second Officer S de Candia were also victims of the attack.

The emergency lifeboat, which had been launched only a few seconds before the ship sank, was taken in charge by the members of the crew, who lit flares to guide the naval ships that were speeding to their rescue. In the faint grey light of the breaking dawn, the boat circled around, picking up survivors who were clinging to rafts and wreckage. A patrol boat arrived and survivors were transferred to the boat, while the remainder were picked up by a destroyer which had been escorting a convoy.

The patrol boat arrived at Fishguard about mid-day and the first batch of survivors was taken to the Seamen's Institute. Some hours later the destroyer put into the port.

In 1986 Sealink Stena Line commissioned a painting of the **St. Patrick** *which was lost off the Pembrokeshire coast during the Second World War. This distinctive picture painted by Colin Morse shows the vessel inward bound from Rosslare off Strumble Head. (Collection of Stena Line at Fishguard)*

ST DAVID (II)

Top right: *First Class Dining Saloon.*

Middle right: *First Class Lounge*

Bottom: *First Class Smoking Room*

Below: *Loading a car at Fishguard the old way during the 1930s.*

(All pictures NRM/ Science and Society Picture Library)

This view shows the **St. Andrew** *(II), the* **Great Western** *and the* **St. David** *(III) at Fishguard in the early 1950s. (National Museums & Galleries of Wales)*

was to continue as a relief vessel in the GWR fleet at both Weymouth and Fishguard in her career. The *St. Patrick* was followed by the Cammell Laird sisters *St. Andrew* (II) and *St. David* (II). The Cammell Laird ships offered good accommodation and had a service speed of 21 knots.

THE SECOND WORLD WAR

On the outbreak of the Second World War, the *St. Andrew* and *St. David* were commandeered by the Crown. Following the *St. Patrick* running for a short spell as a troopship in October 1939, she returned to Fishguard to maintain the route. The Rosslare service was cut back to three days a week during the war years.

During the war, the *St. Andrew* and *St. David* were to see a lot of active service especially at Dunkirk in May 1940, where both ships made several voyages from France to Dover bringing wounded soldiers home. The *St. David* undertook a number of evacuations from Dunkirk in May 1940; the last of these was on 31st May when she was unable to enter the French port due to enemy fire. The *St. Andrew* was employed with evacuations at Cherbourg, Boulogne and Calais prior to being involved in the Dunkirk operation. She later was employed at St Malo.

The two Fishguard 'Saints' were later involved in the Anzio landings on 24th January 1944. The *St. David* was bombed during the landings and sank off the beaches, in spite of being a hospital ship at the time. The ship was quickly engulfed in fire and was sunk with the loss of her Master, Captain Evan Owen and 56 other lives. Her survivors were picked up by the *St. Andrew* which herself was also damaged; in spite of this she

The **St. Andrew** *(II) leaves the Mersey for Fishguard. (Williamson Art Gallery & Museum)*

An interior view of the First Class lounge on board the **St. Andrew**. *(National Museums & Galleries of Wales)*

Side-loading facilities for cars on the **St. David** *were made available on the Fishguard-Rosslare service in 1964 for the first time. This shows a Vauxhall Victor being driven aboard at Fishguard. (National Museums & Galleries of Wales)*

managed to rescue sixty survivors from the *St. David*. Later the *St. Andrew* had to be towed from the Mediterranean to Newport, Monmouthshire for extensive repairs when she hit a mine. It was not until 1947 that she re-opened the service.

Meanwhile, on 13th June 1941, the *St. Patrick* en route from Rosslare was hit by several bombs off Fishguard. So severe was the extent of damage to the ship that she sank in 16 minutes. Thirty lives were lost, including her Master, Captain Faraday. Following the loss of the *St. Patrick* the route was closed until 1947.

A NEW DECADE OF TRAVEL

The Fishguard-Rosslare route re-opened with the *St. Andrew*, on 22nd July 1947, making an overnight sailing from Pembrokeshire under the command of Captain J.J. Kelly. Initially there were three round sailings a week.

Two new ships, bearing the names of their predecessors, were ordered at a cost of £570,000 each to replace the war losses and the new *St. David* (III) entered service on 22nd July 1948, followed by the *St. Patrick* (III) on 4th February 1948. Later during 1948 the *St. Patrick* (III) as she was not required on the route was transferred to Weymouth, where she was to remain until 1964. Following some 16 years at the port she was transferred to the Dover and Folkestone passenger services. She was withdrawn from service in September 1971.

The year 1948 was also to see the nationalisation of the railways in Britain. The impact for the traveller on the Fishguard-Rosslare service was to be very marginal. The Fishguard & Rosslare Railways and Harbours Company was taken over by British Railways; however their operations were little affected by the change and still play an important role

Following the loss of the **St. Patrick** *and the* **St. David** *in the Second World War, the GWR ordered two vessels for Fishguard to replace them. The new* **St. David** *(III) entered service in July 1948. (National Museums & Galleries of Wales)*

today with Stena Line.

The *St. David* and the *St. Andrew* were to remain the mainstays of the Fishguard-Rosslare service until the early-Sixties. It was not until 1961 that daylight sailings were introduced twice a week as an experiment. Such was the success of these daylight sailings in 1961 that they were to continue for the next year but only during the summer period.

With the demand for more car space on the route, British Rail decided to increase the car capacity of one of the 'Saint' class ships. All cars on both sides of the St. George's Channel had to be crane-loaded until 1964. It was therefore decided that the *St. David* would be converted to enable cars to be driven on at the side at both ports. In addition to these improvements to the *St. David*, she would offer more daylight sailings as from 1964. These efforts to improve the operation were to prove a success with over 20.000 cars being carried in 1964 compared with 11,000 during the same period in 1963. At Rosslare, cars still had to be crane-loaded onto flat railway trucks and then unloaded again as there was no road connection at Rosslare Pier until 1965 - it must have been a very frustrating experience for the motorist.

In 1966 British Rail decided to bring in an additional ship for the summer period, to assist the 'Saint' class ships. The cargo ship *Slieve Donard* was brought down from Holyhead to carry cars, whilst passengers were accommodated in the *St. Andrew*.

Looking aft from the bridge wing on board the **St. David** *(III) as she leaves Fishguard Harbour for Rosslare. (Ferry Publications Library)*

ARRIVAL OF THE DUKE

In late Autumn 1966, British Rail announced that the Heysham-Belfast ship *Duke of Rothesay* would be converted to a side-loading ferry for the Fishguard-Rosslare service, in an effort to modernise the fleet at the port and also to offer more car space on the route. Prior to the arrival of the *Duke of Rothesay*, the *St. Andrew* was withdrawn from service at the end of 1966 after 35 years of faithful service.

The *St. David* maintained the winter timetable by herself until the arrival of the *Duke of Rothesay* in May 1967. The *Duke of*

The **St.Patrick** *(III) pictured off Fishguard during her short period at the port, prior to her main career role at Weymouth and then later at Dover and Folkestone. (Martin Lewis collection)*

Rothesay proved very popular with the travelling public, operating with the *St. David*. These two ships were to maintain the route until Spring 1969.

The port of Fishguard still remained rather old-fashioned compared with Holyhead and Stranraer, with side-loading facilities only available. At Holyhead the first drive-on ferry service to the Irish Republic had been opened in 1965 with the *Holyhead Ferry I*; meanwhile at Stranraer the *Antrim Princess* entered service during late 1967, as British Rail's first drive through ferry. Sadly Fishguard was not to offer the same type of port facilities until the early-Seventies.

In early 1969 it was announced that the *Caledonian Princess* would be transferred from Stranraer to join the *Duke of Rothesay* for the summer schedules. The Stranraer vessel had side loading doors cut into her for her role on the St George's Channel as Fishguard did not have a linkspan at the time. Ironically Rosslare had already built a linkspan in 1967 at a cost of £70,000 for the new P&O Normandy Ferries service to Le Havre.

The ageing *St. David* was withdrawn from Fishguard prior to the arrival of the 'Princess'. However, before she was laid up for sale at Holyhead, she was required on the Heysham - Dun Laoghaire service, after a serious fire caused extensive damage to the Britannia tubular bridge across the Menai Straits. As a result of this fire, Holyhead was cut off by rail and so passengers for train connected services to Holyhead had to be transferred to the Lancashire port of Heysham. Following the bridge being repaired and the mailboats' return to Holyhead on 31st January 1971, the *St. David* was sold to Greek owners. The former Fishguard ship sailed from Anglesey on 17th January 1971 renamed *Holyhead*.

During May 1970 the *Caledonian Princess* moved once again to Fishguard, where she was to maintain the service with the

During 1966 the **Slieve Donard** *was used on the route to carry cars to support the* **St. David**. *(Ferry Publications Library)*

Duke of Rothesay until October. While the *Caledonian Princess* was at Fishguard in her second season, she undertook a series of very popular cruises around the Pembrokeshire coastline, which were to be repeated in 1971.

MODERNISATION AT FISHGUARD

During July 1971, British Rail decided to spend £624,000 on providing a linkspan for the port of Fishguard together with major modernisation of the port facilities. The new linkspan would for the first time enable lorries, coaches and caravans to use the route. Sailings for the forthcoming winter and summer season of 1972 would also be increased to cope with the anticipated traffic.

On 6th July 1972 the *Caledonian Princess*, under the command of Captain Dai Griffiths, sailed into Fishguard at the

The **Duke of Rothesay** *was converted to a car ferry in 1974 to replace the* **Caledonian Princess**. *The elegant vessel is seen here departing from Fishguard. (Miles Cowsill)*

FISHGUARD-ROSSLARE

shortest sea route to and from SOUTHERN IRELAND

54miles

LUXURIOUSLY APPOINTED

STEAMERS

EXPRESS

TRAIN SERVICES

FACILITIES FOR CONVEYANCE OF MOTOR CARS

A morning view at Rosslare in 1976 with the **Duke of Lancaster** *at the linkspan. Note in this picture that the breakwater still remains an island away from the mainland and terminal facilities. (Ferry Publications Library)*

The **Preseli** *arrives at Fishguard in the morning sun in 1974 from Rosslare. (Ferry Publications Library)*

opening of the new port facilities by Richard Marsh, Chairman of the British Railways Board. Following the opening of the new terminal facilities, the *Caledonian Princess* continued to enjoy popularity on the route, especially as she could now carry freight and coach traffic on the link. During the winter, she was required to operate only four sailings a week and found it difficult to keep a scheduled crossing time of 3 1/2 hours during bad weather, something many of the ships have had to contend with as the route passage is very exposed to the Atlantic swell and winds.

In March 1973 the *Holyhead Ferry I* relieved on the route for two months, while the *Caledonian Princess* went for major refit and overhaul. In the same month it was announced that a second ship would be introduced to provide space for more cars on the route, as freight traffic increased with the new port facilities at Fishguard and Rosslare. The German-registered freight only vessel *Neckartal* was chartered for an 18-week period and duly arrived at Fishguard on 27th June. She proved to be very successful and she was to remain on the link until November. A near sister to the *Neckartal*, the *Isartal* , was chartered for 1974 and was duly renamed *Preseli* prior to her arrival at the northern Pembrokeshire port.

The summer season in 1974 was to prove fairly eventful. In July the *Caledonian Princess* developed engine trouble which forced her to operate at a reduced speed and it was not until 14th August that the now converted stern-loading ferry *Duke of*

The **Holyhead Ferry I** *relieved on the route for two months in 1973. (Ferry Publications Library)*

A fine view of the **Dover**, *a near sister to the* **Holyhead Ferry I**, *which also relieved on the Rosslare service in the-Seventies. (Ferry Publications Library)*

The **Duke of Lancaster** *leaves Rosslare in 1977 for Fishguard. (Ferry Publications Library)*

The **Maid of Kent** *covered at the port during the refit of the* **Duke of Lancaster** *in 1976. (Ferry Publications Library)*

Rothesay arrived at Fishguard to stand in for the 'Princess'. While the *Caledonian Princess* was undergoing repairs, disaster hit the *Duke of Rothesay* on 24th September when she collided with a barge whilst docking in heavy seas at Rosslare. On the same day, during very high winds, the *Preseli* took 13 1/2 hours to complete the 54-mile crossing between Ireland and Pembrokeshire. The *Caledonian Princess* returned to Fishguard on 29th October following repairs to her engines and a short spell at Weymouth on relief duties.

During the autumn, Sealink announced that the *Avalon* would be converted to a car ferry for the Fishguard-Rosslare service at a cost of £1 million. The Harwich-based vessel was one of Sealink's most luxurious ships at the time, operating not only on the Dutch service but also carrying out a series of European cruises each year. When converted she would be able to provide accommodation for 1,200 passengers and 210 cars.

The *Caledonian Princess* made her final farewell from the Fishguard service on 19th June 1975 and prior to the arrival of the *Avalon* the *Duke of Lancaster* stood in at the port.

The *Avalon* was to prove to be a great success and remained on the Pembrokeshire link until 2nd January 1976, when she was transferred to the Holyhead route. Her place was taken by the *Dover* until June, when the former Harwich ship returned again for the summer schedules.

During the New Year in 1977, Sealink announced cutbacks on the Irish services, in an effort to save money on both the Fishguard and Holyhead routes. As far as Fishguard-Rosslare was concerned these cutbacks were to take place in four stages.

The former Harwich-based ship the **Avalon** *was converted to a car ferry in 1976. This wonderful profile of her sees her leaving Fishguard for Rosslare during her first season. (Ferry Publications Library)*

CALEDONIAN PRINCESS

Top: *The* **Caledonian Princess** *departs from Fishguard during her first season on the route. (Ferry Publications Library)*

Above: *The First Class Smokeroom on the* **Caledonian Princess.** *(NRM/Science and Society Picture Library)*

Opposite page top: *The main lounge on the Promenade Deck was the largest of the Second Class areas on board the* **Caledonian Princess**. *(NRM/Science and Society Picture Library)*

Opposite page middle: *This view shows the Second Class Cafeteria with one of the 25 feet long murals designed by David Gentleman. (NRM/Science and Society Picture Library)*

Opposite page bottom: *The First Class Resturant could seat up to 50 passengers.(NRM/Science and Society Picture Library)*

The **Caledonian Princess** *arrives at Fishguard following the opening on the new linkspan at the port in July 1972. (Ferry Publications Library)*

The two Stena sisters together at Fishguard. The **Stena Normandica** *(later renamed* **St. Brendan***) is at the linkspan with the* **Stena Nordica** *astern of her in 1980. (Miles Cowsill)*

Stage 1 - from 1st January to 18th June and from 10th October until the end of the year, the *Avalon* and the *Duke of Lancaster* would operate a one class service. Stage 2 - the freight-only vessel *Anderida* would from 7th April to 1st May operate a freight-only service, as the *Duke of Lancaster* had little freight capacity. Stage 3 as from 2nd May the *Anderida* and the *Avalon* would operate together one trip a day each. The final stage, from October, was to re-schedule the timings of the ships to help motorists, foot passengers and freight drivers.

Surprisingly, prior to Christmas in 1977, Sealink announced expansion plans for Fishguard which would involve transferring the *Lord Warden* from Dover. For an eight-week period during the summer the *Lord Warden* would provide an extra round sailing between Fishguard and Rosslare and in addition to this a new peak season link from Fishguard to Dun Laoghaire would be opened. Departure times on the new link were 08.00 from Pembrokeshire with an inward sailing from Ireland at 15.00. Traffic on the new service was slow to develop; however, by the end of July bookings were showing very encouraging signs.

A SWEDISH CAR FERRY

With the threat of a new rival service between Rosslare and Pembroke Dock operated by B&I, Stena Line's *Stena Nordica* underwent berthing trials at Fishguard on 14th September 1978. The Swedish ship was considered ideal for this route, with a capacity for 470 cars and 1,400 passengers. The introduction of such a ferry would mean that only one-ship operation would be required in the future. Following the successful berthing trials of the 'Nordica', Sealink announced that they were ordering from Harland & Wolff at Belfast a new ship for the port, its first new tonnage since 1947. The new £16 million ferry would allow the *Avalon* to be switched to Holyhead and the *Anderida* to return to Dover.

In early January 1979 the company decided not to operate the Fishguard-Dun Laoghaire service for the following season, as Holyhead were concerned about the effect that it would have upon their own service.

On 3rd March, Sealink then announced that the sister to the *Stena Nordica*, the *Stena Normandica*, would be chartered for a 19 month period until the arrival of the new ship from Belfast. The arrival of the *Stena Normandica* on 3rd April brought a sudden significant change to the link. Prior to her arrival at Fishguard, she had seen a variety of charter operations since being built for Stena Line in 1974 in Germany. The sheer size and capacity of this vessel had never been seen at Fishguard; however, compared with other UK and European ferry operations at the time, the *Stena Normandica* was not really a very large vessel. For some unknown reason the *Stena Normandica* entered service with her own distinctive livery, different from other Sealink vessels in the fleet, with an all-white hull and upperworks and the word 'Sealink' in blue on the hull. On the arrival of the chartered Swedish ship, the *Avalon* sailed north to Holyhead.

By the early summer, the company were claiming that the passenger and freight figures were up by some 10% since the introduction of the new ship. Sadly the *Stena Normandica* encountered mechanical problems during the summer, which eventually meant that the *Avalon* had to return to Fishguard while the *Stena Normandica* underwent major engine repairs. The 'Normandica' returned to service again in September.

During mid-February 1980, the sister to the *Stena*

The **Lord Warden** *maintained the Fishguard-Dun Laoghaire and Rosslare service in 1978. (Ferry Publications Library)*

This interesting view shows the **Stena Normandica** *prior to her departure for overhaul with the* **St. Columba** *ready to take her place on the route in February 1982. (Miles Cowsill)*

Normandica, the *Stena Nordica,* returned to Fishguard while her sister was sent for an overhaul. While the *Stena Normandica* was away on refit, she had a side door fitted to enable her to load and unload cars by the starboard side at Fishguard to speed up operations. By mid-summer Sealink were expressing interest in purchasing the *Stena Normandica,* as the company were impressed with her performance and it was also now speculated that the new ferry being built for Fishguard (unofficially named *St. David*) might now be used at Holyhead with the *St. Columba*.

In December the charter of the *Stena Normandica* was extended to enable the *St. David* to be utilised the next summer on the Holyhead route.

As work was nearing completion at Belfast on the *St. Christopher* (a sister ship to the *St. David*) for the Dover-Calais service, it was becoming increasingly certain that she would make her debut on the Fishguard-Rosslare service, as the *Stena Normandica* had to be slotted in for an urgent refit. Dover were naturally very disappointed when the company announced that the *St. Christopher* would make her maiden voyage between Wales and Ireland. She left Harland & Wolff on 14th March for berthing trials at Rosslare.

The *St. Christopher* in fact did not make her maiden voyage on the Fishguard-Rosslare service, as the *St. Columba* broke down and the new ship had to sail direct from Rosslare after trials to stand in for the troubled Danish built vessel on the Holyhead-Dun Laoghaire link.

On 19th March, the *St. Christopher* eventually was able to relieve the *Stena Normandica* on the 14.45 sailing to Ireland. The *St. Christopher* was to prove an excellent vessel whilst at Fishguard, especially during some very inclement weather at the start of April. The *Stena Normandica* returned to her home port on 13th April to allow the *St. Christopher* to sail south to join her sister the *St. Anselm* on the 'Flagship Service'.

During the next overhaul period, industrial action at Holyhead delayed another new visitor to Pembrokeshire, the *St. Columba*. Holyhead were not happy that their flagship was going to the rival Irish Sea port as they were worried that their vessel might not return to North Wales, because the new *St. David* was proving to be a popular and efficient ship on the link. Following assurances from the management at Holyhead in late February, the *St. Columba* came south to release the *Stena Normandica*.

In late February 1983, the *Stena Normandica* went off for refit at Swansea and the *St. David* made her first visit to Fishguard. Following the *Stena Normandica* returning to service she

The **Stena Normandica** *arrives at Rosslare in the late evening light in September 1980 from Fishguard. (Miles Cowsill)*

The **Stena Normandica** *leaves Fishguard in her new Sealink livery prior to privatisation of the company. (Miles Cowsill)*

Fresh from overhaul, the **St Brendan** *proudly presents the new livery of Sealink British Ferries in 1984. (Miles Cowsill collection)*

promptly broke down; as luck would have it the *St. Anselm* was sailing down the Irish Sea back to Dover following her major overhaul at Belfast. She hastily took up the run on 28th March for two days, until the *Stena Normandica* was operational once again.

PRIVATISATION

With the forthcoming sale of Sealink by the Government in Summer 1984, the *Stena Normandica* sailed to Falmouth for her refit and reappeared in the company's new livery and image for privatisation. During July 1984 Sealink UK Limited was purchased for £66 million by the Bermuda-based Sea Containers Limited, the company in future was to be branded as Sealink British Ferries..

During early February 1985, Sealink British Ferries and B&I Line announced that they had concluded discussions aimed at solving the new over-capacity on the Irish Sea. Talks had started in December against a background of achieving savings for both rival companies and bringing frequency of service more in line with demand.

Certain reductions on daylight sailings were made at Fishguard, while B&I Line's Rosslare-Pembroke Dock service was suspended during the company's overhaul programme and traffic was transferred to the North Pembrokeshire port under the terms of the agreement.

On 15th April, Sealink British Ferries acquired the *Stena Normandica* from Stena Line and shortly afterwards she was renamed the *St. Brendan*. The newly-purchased ferry was named after one of the most colourful Irish saints, who had a long and famous association with the sea. Saint Brendan is most renowned for his seven-year voyage to North America which, it is alleged,he was the first to discover.

By the end of the summer the future of B&I's Rosslare-Pembroke Dock service was very much in doubt especially with the pooling arrangement with Sealink.

Meanwhile the *St. Brendan* encountered more engine problems at the end of September. B&I put on extra sailings at their end to try to relieve the build-up of freight at Fishguard.

The **St. Christopher** *goes astern at Fishguard during her short spell on the route in April 1981. (Miles Cowsill)*

The **St. David** *was originally planned as the flagship vessel for the Fishguard-Rosslare route but with the overwhelming success of the* **Stena Normandica** *she was placed on the Holyhead-Dun Laoghaire route. She is seen here during her first visit to Fishguard in March 1983. (Miles Cowsill)*

When it was realised that the ex-Swedish ship's problems were fairly major, it was decided to send the *Hengist* round from Folkestone to Fishguard to stand in for the *St. Brendan* whilst she underwent repairs and an early refit. The former Swedish ferry returned to the route in mid-November.

During October Sealink British Ferries announced that they had revised their agreement with B&I Line. The major change as far as the St. George's Channel services were concerned was the closure of the Rosslare-Pembroke Dock route with a loss of 535 jobs. At Fishguard, Sealink British Ferries agreed to introduce a 'new jumbo ferry' which was rumoured at the time to be the *Peter Pan* from TT Line of Germany. Like all good rumours in the shipping world the *Peter Pan* never came around the breakwater at Fishguard. The long-established Fishguard-Rosslare link was favoured by the public and freight hauliers in preference to the Pembroke Dock link; it was not only shorter than B&I Line's service, but provided a larger modern ship with superior facilities. B&I sadly had no-one but themselves to blame for the rundown of their new link, as they had failed to invest in suitable tonnage for the service since its advent in

As part of the joint agreement between Sealink and B&I, the **St. Brendan** *was re-painted in a joint livery. She is seen here in 1987 outward bound for Rosslare. (Miles Cowsill)*

The **Hengist**, *formerly a Folkestone-based vessel, is pictured here outward bound from Fishguard whilst relieving on the route. (Miles Cowsill)*

Following the charter of the **Prins Philippe**, *the Irish-registered vessel* **Innisfallen** *maintained the Fishguard-Rosslare service for the rest of the 1986 summer season. (Miles Cowsill)*

The Folkestone-based ship **Vortigern** *is seen here arriving at Fishguard covering for the refit of the* **Stena Normandica** *in 1987. (Miles Cowsill)*

1980.

The Pembroke Dock service closed on Sunday 5th January 1986 with the 02.15 service to Rosslare. The closure of the link was a major blow for the economy and for the tourist trade of South Pembrokeshire with Ireland.Sealink British Ferries made worldwide enquiries for their new jumbo ship to replace the *St. Brendan*, but the company were admitting by the early summer that they were finding it difficult to find such a ship for the service. As a result of the company failing to find a replacement for the *St. Brendan*, it was decided under the pooling arrangement with B&I that the *Innisfallen* would undertake extra sailings to meet the demand on the Southern Corridor. Initially the *Innisfallen* could not be released, as she was required elsewhere in the B&I fleet to cover for overhauls on the Liverpool and Holyhead services, and therefore the Belgian ferry *Prins Philippe* was chartered from RMT for three weeks. Following the *Innisfallen's* spell at Fishguard, she was sold to Strintzis Lines for further service in the Mediterranean.

During the New Year, the *St. Brendan* was due to be relieved by B&I's *Leinster* under the pooling arrangement with the Irish company. B&I at the time were faced with a major industrial dispute within their company which prevented the *Leinster* from coming to Fishguard. Sealink were forced to change their plans and the multi-purpose ferry *Vortigern* was sent from Folkestone instead to cover for the refit.

Whilst the *St. Brendan* was away on overhaul she received another new livery, incorporating that of both Sealink British Ferries and B&I. This livery was to last only one year and at the time was much resented by Sealink staff on both sides of the St. George's Channel. In 1987, as in the previous year, a second ship was required for the peak season and B&I chartered the French ferry *Senlac* from Sealink Dieppe Ferries. She commenced her summer season on the Irish Sea on 18th June offering one round sailing to support the *St. Brendan*; the one sailing subsequently increased during late July to two round sailings. The smart looking *Senlac* proved a popular partner to the *St. Brendan* and would have been an ideal long-term purchase for the link. B&I tried to purchase her; however, by the time the Irish company became interested in the vessel, she had been sold by SNCF for service in the Mediterranean.

Like the previous year, Fishguard was being served by an Inter-City 125 service from London Paddington in an effort to offer a better service to passengers. On the other side of the Irish Sea, it was announced during 1986 that IR £5.3million was to

The **Prins Philippe** *was chartered by B&I Line as part of the joint arrangement with Sealink in 1986 to offer additional capacity on the link. (FotoFlite)*

The **Horsa** *covered for the refit of the* **St. Brendan** *in 1984. She is pictured here leaving Dun Laoghaire for Holyhead in 1990. (Miles Cowsill)*

In 1987 as part of the joint agreement between Sealink and B&I, the French-registered **Senlac** *was chartered to offer additional capacity on the Fishguard-Rosslare route. (Miles Cowsill)*

be spent on improving the port facilities at Rosslare. At the end of 1987 B&I withdrew from the pooling agreement with Sealink. As a result of their decision, the Irish company returned to their former UK port of Pembroke Dock.The winter refit for the *St. Brendan* saw the vessel sailing north to the Mersey in March 1987. The *St. David* was sent from Stranraer to deputise while the *St. Brendan* underwent her overhaul. Engine problems were to plague the *St. Brendan* during the spring, and in April the *Earl Harold* stood in for her while repairs were undertaken to the 'Brendan'. Following these repairs she broke down again on 18th May 1988, and this time the *Darnia* had to be sent from Scotland to stand in for her, while repairs were undertaken to her variable-pitch propellers.

During August the freight vessel *Stena Sailer* was moved from Holyhead to back up the *St. Brendan* for the peak season to move freight. In October, the *Earl Harold* was back on the Pembrokeshire link, so that the 'Brendan' could go off for further engine repairs prior to the winter With these repairs taking longer than planned the *Cambridge Ferry* was sent up from Dover to support the *Earl Harold*. The *St. Brendan* returned to the link in December, and as traffic levels had reached an all time high prior to Christmas the Dover vessel was retained until the end of year.

Meanwhile it was announced that the *St. Anselm* would be transferred from Dover to Fishguard at an early date, to enable the *St. Brendan* to open a possible new service for the company from Southampton to Cherbourg. In the event neither plan materialised. The level of freight on the link had increased to such an extent that Sealink decided that an additional vessel would have to be brought in on the link to support the *St.*

This view shows the **Visby** *leaving her home port prior to being transferred and chartered to Sealink British Ferries. (Miles Cowsill Collection)*

The **St Brendan** *is pictured here in Sealink British Ferries' livery following the privatisation of Sealink in 1984. (Miles Cowsill)*

FELICITY

The **Felicity** *was chartered by Sealink British Ferries for the Fishguard-Rosslare route in early 1990. After modifications at Tilbury, she was, in March 1990, introduced on the Fishguard-Rosslare route. Later in 1990 she was renamed* **Stena Felicity**. *In Summer 1997 she was returned to Rederi AB Gotland for re-building, prior to her entry into service with Destination Gotland in 1998. She was renamed* **Visby** *once again. In late 2002 she was renamed* **Visborg**. *In March 2003 she was replaced by new tonnage on the service from mainland Sweden to Gotland. In June 2003 she was sold to Polferries, renamed* **Scandinavia** *and placed on their Gdansk-Nynashamn route. The top view shows the* **Felicity** *on her delivery voyage to Fishguard from Dunkirk. Above view shows her cafeteria, above right her cinema and bottom right her luxuriously-appointed restaurant. (FotoFlite/Miles Cowsill)*

Originally built as the **Ailsa Princess** *and later renamed* **Earl Harold**, *the former Stranraer vessel was to cover for the absence of the* **St. Brendan** *in 1988. She is seen here swinging off the berth at Fishguard. (Miles Cowsill)*

Brendan for the summer, so the veteran train ferry *Cambridge Ferry* was brought in again. The *Cambridge Ferry* proved to be a popular freight vessel on the link until early January 1990, when she was sent to Milford Haven to lay up with the company's *Earl William*.

FISHGUARD'S BIGGEST

On 4th September 1989, plans were unveiled by Sealink British Ferries to introduce the largest and most luxurious ferry ever seen on the Irish Sea services. Following extensive negotiations with Gotland Line, the company secured a five-year charter of the *Visby* to replace the *St. Brendan*. The *Visby* (15,001 gross tons) had originally been built for Gotland Line for a service between Nynashamn (south of Stockholm) and Visby, capital of the island of Gotland. The Swedish ship would have a capacity for 2,000 passengers, 517 cars or 54 freight units, or a mixture. Following the announcement that Fishguard were at last going to have their new jumbo ferry, work commenced on improving the port facilities at both Fishguard and Rosslare.

Meanwhile, it was disclosed that the *St. Brendan* had been sold to Navarma of Italy, later branded as Moby Lines, for service in the Mediterranean. The sale of the *St. Brendan* came as rather a surprise in the light of Sealink wanting new tonnage for their own fleet to replace four of their Sixties-built ships. At the time of the announcement by Sealink, it was thought that the Fishguard ship would be transferred to the Portsmouth-Cherbourg service to incease capacity on the link or possibly to Stranraer.

As Fishguard moved into the Nineties, the *St. Brendan* experienced some of the worst weather of her career at the port. On 25th January 1990, winds of up to 115 m.p.h. were experienced on the Irish Sea, followed by nearly a three week spell of further strong gales. During this very inclement weather, the *St. Brendan* battled through some of the worst seas for many decades, operating at times when other services on the Irish Sea were cancelled .

While the 'Brendan' was coping with the weather, the *Visby* slipped into Tilbury from Sweden to undergo modifications and improvements to her passenger areas costing some £2 million, prior to entering service. Following her refit at Tilbury, due to the Officers' Union and the management failing to reach agreement on a new working pattern for the vessel, she sailed sailed to Dunkirk for lay-up following her refit. Eventually the *Felicity* arrived at Fishguard on 2nd March 1990 at 17.00 for berthing trials. The Swedish vessel had undertaken trials earlier in the day at Rosslare, en route from Dunkirk. She entered commercial service on Monday 5th March on the 15.00 sailing from Fishguard; meanwhile the *St. Brendan* undertook her last official sailing for the company inward on the Sunday from Rosslare on the 21.40 sailing. Following the *St. Brendan* destoring, she was handed over to her new Italian owners the next day. Her new owners, Moby Lines, renamed her the *Moby Vincent* and she left the following week from Fishguard for her new role in Italy. Currently she operates between Livorno and Bastia.

The **Stena Felicity** *leaving Rosslare for Fishguard in her Stena Sealink Line livery. (Miles Cowsill)*

STENA LINE ERA

The *Felicity* soon settled down into a regular roster between the two ports. However, sadly her first season was marred by two minor technical problems which interrupted operations. The second of these saw the vessel having to be taken out of service and her place being taken by the *Horsa* from Holyhead.

Sealink Stena Line announced in the autumn of 1990 that they planned to invest something in the region of £4.5 million in the port of Fishguard to improve port facilities and infrastructure. As a result of the takeover of Sealink British Ferries by Stena Line of Sweden, the Fishguard vessel was subsequently renamed *Stena Felicity*.

The *Cambridge Ferry* which had been operating in tandem with the *St. Brendan* during peak periods stood down on the arrival of the *Felicity*; however, she was required again during the Christmas of 1990 to support the 'Felicity'. The veteran train ferry was to remain at Fishguard for the following year as additional back up to the conventional passenger ship with the continued growth in freight traffic.

On 17th November 1990 the *Stena Cambria* (ex *St.Anselm*) arrived at Fishguard to allow the *Felicity* to undergo her overhaul at Falmouth. The *Stena Cambria* took up the 15.00 sailing to Rosslare, heralding a new era as far as Sealink was concerned as the first ship to operate in the new Sealink Stena Line livery. During the overhaul of the *Felicity* further improvements were carried out to her passenger areas, including a new bar. She was renamed *Stena Felicity* and was due to re-enter service again during early December, but due to very inclement weather she was unable to dock at Fishguard. The exceptionally high winds and rough seas also prevented the *Stena Cambria* from docking on the same day and she was forced to take shelter in Cardigan Bay until the next day. The *Stena Felicity* eventually was able to dock at Fishguard and took up the 15.00 sailing on the Sunday, allowing the 'Cambria' to leave the route.

Once again the *Cambridge Ferry* emerged from lay-up at Milford Haven on 18th December to operate in tandem with the *Stena Felicity* during the busy Christmas period. On 27th December the 'Felicity' carried 516 cars on the 15.00 sailing to Rosslare - a port record to date. The *Cambridge Ferry* returned to Milford Haven on the morning of Christmas Eve following her short period supporting freight operations on the route. She returned again for six weeks at the end of July 1991 to support the *Stena Felicity* again. In November 1992 the 'Felicity' once again went for refit and her place was taken by the *Stena Cambria*. With further changes in the Sealink operation the vessel returned in a further new livery, that of Stena Sealink Line.

During the winter period of 1994 the *Stena Felicity* went for overhaul and her place was taken by the chartered *Norrona*.

FAST FERRY SERVICE

The success of the fast craft operations between Holyhead and Dun Laoghaire with the *Stena Sea Lynx* saw the transfer of this vessel to Fishguard to open a new fast ferry service between Pembrokeshire and Southern Ireland. The new operation allowed for three sailings a day in each direction as from 14th June until 22nd July 1994 when the schedule was increased to

The **Stena Cambria** *(ex* **St Anselm***) first visited Fishguard in 1990. She is seen here arriving at the port following her renaming. (Miles Cowsill)*

Smyrill Line's **Norrona** *covered for the refit of the* **Stena Felicity** *in 1994. (Miles Cowsill)*

five round sailings a day. The introduction of the new fastcraft operation created some 40 new jobs at Fishguard and was to be an immediate success with travellers. Not only did it allow for the day-trip market to Ireland to expand with much more convenient sailing times from the Welsh side for passengers to enjoy excursions to Southern Ireland and Wexford but it was also eventually to create a new market in the opposite direction with the very successful Pembrokeshire-based theme park of Oakwood for Irish visitors.

The new port facilities at Fishguard were opened by the Secretary of State for Wales, John Redwood, on Wednesday 14th July 1994.

The success of the *Stena Sea Lynx* was such that the carryings on the route had increased by some 8% by the end of August 1994 compared with the same period the previous year and over the whole of 1994 freight was to grow by some 3% on the Southern Corridor.

At the end of September the *Stena Felicity* had to be withdrawn from operations following the *Estonia* disaster in the Baltic, for checks to her bow door. When it was found that the vessel required repairs to her bow door she was sent to Falmouth. With the absence of the *Stena Felicity* the *Stena Sea Lynx* schedules were increased to four round sailings a day and the freight vessel *Vinzia E* was brought in to support freight operations. The 'Felicity' did not return to the route until 15th October when she entered service again with restricted operations. She was not able to operate in seas over 4 metres, which was to cause major problems during the winter period. On 11th November the MSA (Marine Safety Agency) withdrew the passenger certificate of the *Stena Felicity* on the same day that the Swedish authorities gave the all-clear for the ship to operate in over 4 metre seas. As a result of her passenger certificate being withdrawn, she was forced to operate as a freight-only vessel until 18th November. The *Stena Sea Lynx II* was transferred from Holyhead to cover for the absence of the 'Felicity' but due to the inclement weather she was only able to do five sailings during her five days at the port. Eventually these restrictions were lifted following further investigations and repairs.

The **Cambridge Ferry** *first came to the Fishguard service in 1989. She is seen here in her livery which was used whilst operating on the English Channel and North Sea routes. (Miles Cowsill)*

STENA FELICITY

The **Stena Felicity** *is seen here arriving from Rosslare in June 1992. (Miles Cowsill)*

An early morning view of the **Stena Sea Lynx** *leaving Rosslare for Fishguard in June 1997. (Miles Cowsill)*

The **Condor 10** *was chartered by Stena Line to maintain the fast ferry service in 1996. The Incat craft is seen here arriving at Fishguard. (Miles Cowsill)*

Early Spring 1995 saw the Stena Line management considering the transfer of the *Stena Jutlandica* for the following year from the Gothenburg-Frederikshavn service to replace the chartered *Stena Felicity*, whose contract was due to end the following March. In the event these plans did not materialise however, had the 'Jutlandica' been transferred from Scandinavia it could possibly have seen her operating three round sailings a day on the route.

On 11th February 1995 the *Stena Felicity* was sent to Swansea for a short overhaul, her place being taken by the *Stena Antrim*. The *Stena Sea Lynx* had another excellent season in 1995 carrying nearly 37% of the total passenger traffic between Fishguard and Rosslare. At the end of her season on the route on 15th October she was transferred to Holyhead to maintain their fast ferry service until the end of the month. A further year's charter of the *Stena Felicity* was secured by Stena Line in the latter part of 1995. It was anticipated that her charter thereafter would not be renewed and that the *Stena Europe* from Harwich would be transferred to the link.

On 3rd April the *Stena Felicity* left Fishguard for overhaul in Germany; her place was taken by the *Stena Londoner*.

It had originally been planned that the *Stena Sea Lynx* would maintain the fast ferry operation on the route for 1996. However, this particular fast craft was not made available and the Swedish company chartered the much-travelled *Condor 10* to maintain the route. This vessel had originally operated between Weymouth and the Channel Islands and thereafter had seen a series of charters worldwide, including Scandinavia and New Zealand. The *Condor 10* entered service on 17th May and maintained the route during the summer extremely reliably without any major technical problems.

ENTER THE QUEEN

During Autumn 1996 Stena Line announced that the *Stena Felicity* would be withdrawn from service as from 31st March 1997. At the time of the announcement no replacement vessel was named. However, with the forthcoming introduction of the fast ferry service between Harwich and the Hook of Holland it was becoming clear that the prime contender for the route would be either the *Stena Europe* or the *Koningin Beatrix*. On 6th November Stena Line announced that the largest and most luxurious ferry in the fleet would be switched the following spring from the Hook of Holland-Harwich service to the

The **Vinzia E** *was used on the Fishguard-Rosslare route in March 1994. (Miles Cowsill)*

The much-travelled **Stena Londoner** *leaves the port of Fishguard during the overhaul period of the* **Stena Felicity** *in 1996. (Miles Cowsill)*

This view of the **Stena Felicity** *shows her leaving the port of Fishguard as the* **Stena Lynx** *arrives from Rosslare. (John Bryant)*

Fishguard route. The *Koningin Beatrix*, 31,189 tonnes with a passenger capacity for 2,100, would replace the *Stena Felicity.*

Commenting on the introduction of the *Koningin Beatrix* on the route following the announcement, Nick Saul, Stena Line's Shipping and Port Manager at Fishguard, said; "A number of options have been considered as replacements for the route and I could not have wished for better news than this. Our present ferry is very large and well appointed by any standards but the *Koningin Beatrix* is in a league of her own. Alongside our fast catamaran on the route, we will be able to raise levels of quality and customer choice to new heights."

On the introduction of the *Stena Discovery* (HSS) on the Harwich-Hook of Holland service, the *Koningin Beatrix* stood

The **Stena Cambria** *is seen here at Fishguard covering for the refit of the* **Koningin Beatrix** *in 1998. (Miles Cowsill)*

down on the route. Prior to her transfer to the Southern Corridor she undertook a short charter as an accommodation ship in Amsterdam. On Thursday 19th June 1997 the former Dutch vessel was re-registered in London with an official ceremony held later the same day to change the Dutch flag to the British flag. However, following the ceremony the Red Ensign was replaced by the Dutch flag following a dispute between Stena Line and a Dutch bank. As a result she sailed from the Hook of Holland on Saturday 21st June at 18.00 with the port of registry of London on her stern, flying the Dutch flag with both a Dutch and a British Captain, an unusual situation which eventually was resolved.

The *Koningin Beatrix* arrived at Rosslare at 10.16 on 22nd June under the command of Captain Roy Forsyth, the Senior Master at Fishguard and a Dutch Captain. Following undertaking berthing trials it was planned that she would then sail from Rosslare to Fishguard to take up the 18.00 sailing to Ireland on 25th June.

During the latter part of June 1997 there was some very inclement weather which resulted in the fastcraft operations being cancelled and some other rival operations also closed, resulting in chaos at the port of Fishguard. It was decided that the *Koningin Beatrix* would enter commercial service in tandem with the *Stena Felicity* in an effort to clear this backlog. Because of the bad weather the Dutch ship was sent to Pembroke Dock where there was more shelter to undertake berthing trials. The *Koningin Beatrix* undertook those trials on 27th June at 11.30 at Pembroke Dock and then entered operations for the first time on the Irish Sea on a non-scheduled 14.30 sailing to Rosslare. The gales were so strong in the Milford Haven estuary that she had to have two tugs to get her off the berth; some 20 minutes

KONINGIN BEATRIX

Originally the **Koningin Beatrix** *was built for Crown Line in the Netherlands for their Hook of Holland-Harwich service. In 1989 the vessel was transferred to the ownership of Stena Line bv. In June 1997 she was placed on the Fishguard service and two months later she was transferred to the British flag. In 2001 she was transferred onto Stena Line's operation between Karlskrona and Gdynia and renamed* **Stena Baltica**. *In Spring 2005 she was rebuilt to increase her freight capacity. The top view shows the* **Koningin Beatrix** *swinging off the berth at Fishguard during her first week in service. The right-hand view shows the* **Koningin Beatrix** *outward bound from the Hook of Holland in the earlier Stena Line livery. The photo below shows the vessel in her Crown Line livery. (Miles Cowsill/Ferry Publications Library)*

This unusual view shows the **Stena Felicity** *at Pembroke Dock. The vessel was forced to use the port of Pembroke Dock during her last few days in service on the Southern Corridor due to inclement weather. (Miles Cowsill)*

after the *Koningin Beatrix* left Pembroke Dock the *Stena Felicity* berthed for the first time at that port.

Eventually the bad weather subsided and the *Stena Felicity* completed her last voyage on the Southern Corridor on 25th June, not to Fishguard from Rosslare but to Pembroke Dock. Meanwhile, the *Koningin Beatrix* made her first official sailing on the Fishguard-Rosslare service on 3rd July on a re-scheduled 15.00 sailing at 20.00 to Ireland.

On 14th August the *Koningin Beatrix* was eventually officially re-flagged under the British Ensign.

The *Koningin Beatrix* was due to go to refit in early January 1998 and to be replaced by the Stranraer-based vessel *Stena Caledonia*, which was due to remain at Fishguard until 23rd January. The problems at Harwich with the *Stena Discovery* saw her having to be withdrawn and her place being taken by the *Stena Voyager* from Stranraer. As a result of this transfer the *Stena Caledonia* had to sail north again to cover the Stranraer-Belfast service. The 'Caledonia' was replaced by the *Stena Cambria* from Dover as a substitute vessel in place of the *Koningin Beatrix*.

The *Stena Lynx* once again returned to Fishguard on 28th April to cover for the fast ferry operation on the Southern Corridor.

In July 1998 Stena Line was the official maritime carrier for the prestigious Tour de France. Following completion of the first stage of the tour in Ireland, the *Koningin Beatrix* and the *Stena Challenger* (from Holyhead) were chartered to sail from Cork to Roscoff with part of the support teams and their crews, whilst the *Stena Caledonia* was employed to sail from Rosslare to Roscoff. All three ships carried over 2,000 tour personnel, TV crews and media, as well as hundreds of cars, vans and lorries. The *European Pathfinder* was chartered by Stena Line to undertake a round trip between Rosslare and Fishguard to move freight in the absence of the *Koningin Beatrix*.

Meanwhile, the 74-metre Incat craft *Stena Lynx* was returned to her owners in early December and was replaced by the larger *Stena Lynx III* (ex *Elite*) for the following season. The larger InCat would provide increased capacity on the route with space for 140 cars and 620 passengers.

During the winter of 1999 the *Koningin Beatrix* refitted between 16th and 28th February and her place was taken by the *Stena Caledonia* from Stranraer. Once again during the 'Beatrix' refit, the *Stena Caledonia* had to be called back to Stranraer as there were problems with the fast craft *Stena Voyager* on the route. Her place was taken by the *Rosebay* from the Harwich-Hook of Holland service from 22nd February. She was to remain on the Fishguard-Rosslare service until 12th March when her place was taken by the *Stena Lynx III*. With problems also at Holyhead the *Koningin Beatrix* did not return immediately to the

The veteran train ferry **Cambridge Ferry** *leaves Rosslare on her morning sailing to Fishguard whilst supporting the* **Stena Felicity** *on the route in 1996. (Miles Cowsill)*

Stena Lynx III
LYNX
Stena Line

An evening view at Rosslare with the **Stena Lynx III** *at her berth pending her early evening departure to Pembrokeshire and the* **Koningin Beatrix** *having just arrived from Fishguard. (Miles Cowsill)*

Stena Line's **Rosebay** *was sent from Harwich to cover on the route in 1999 during the absence of the* **Koningin Beatrix**. *The vessel is seen here turning off the berth at Fishguard. (Miles Cowsill)*

Fishguard service but was placed on the Holyhead-Dublin route between 5th and 12th March. She re-entered service some four days later on the Southern Corridor.

Following the arrival of the *Stena Lynx III* at Fishguard, the service was re-launched on 22nd April 1999. At the launch Stena Line's President, Bo Severed, underlined the company's commitment to maintaining its market leadership on the Irish Sea. At the press conference Mr Severed further added: "The 40 knot *Stena Lynx III* will increase the fast ferry capacity on the route by some 30% in conjunction with the *Koningin Beatrix*. The arrival of the *Stena Lynx III* provides us with a superior fast craft which now fully complements the Stena HSS operations of ours at Holyhead and Stranraer."

In 1999 there was speculation that the *Koningin Beatrix* might be replaced by another ship within the fleet. With the increased passenger and car carryings on the fast ferry operation and also a drop in freight on the link it was suggested that the vessel might possibly be moved to the Baltic where she would be more suited with such a high capacity of cabins.

During the winter of 2000 the *Koningin Beatrix* was replaced by the *Stena Invicta* from Holyhead from 7th February. The former Dover vessel, which had been laid up at Zeebrugge, remained on the route until 16th March as the 'Beatrix' was also required to cover for the *Stena Challenger's* refit on the Holyhead-Dublin route. On 24th March Stena Line announced that they planned to reduce the operational season of the fast ferry service on the Southern Corridor in an effort to save costs. In spite of this announcement the fast ferry operation continued to attract good levels of traffic.

The *Koningin Beatrix* overhauled between 7th and 12th

This view shows the **Stena Caledonia** *(ex* **St. David***) at Rosslare covering for the refit of the* **Stena Europe** *in 2005. (Gordon Hislip)*

An interesting view of the **Koningin Beatrix** *and the* **Stena Galloway** *during 2001. The* **Stena Galloway** *had just taken up on the route to allow the* **Koningin Beatrix** *to go for repairs. (Mike O'Brian)*

January 2001 when no replacement vessel ran in her absence, this was the first time the route closed during an overhaul period. In spite of the reduction of the fast ferry operation the previous year, carryings on the route continued to grow. During the period January to September 2000 carryings amounted to 721,000 passengers and 164,000 cars, compared with the same period the previous year when only 697,000 passengers used the route.

During the summer of 2001 the *Koningin Beatrix* suffered with a series of engine problems, which meant she had to operate at a slower speed. Eventually the Dutch vessel had to be withdrawn from service in early September to allow her to go for essential repairs and early overhaul at Brest in France. During these repairs she was blown off the quay and experienced extensive damage, which further delayed her return to the Southern Corridor. Her place was taken by the *Stena Galloway* from Stranraer, which remained on the route until 31st October.

FURTHER CHANGES

At the end of the year it was announced that the *Koningin Beatrix* would be transferred to the company's Poland-Sweden service as from March 2002. The vessel currently operating the link, the *Stena Europe*, would be switched to the Southern Corridor. Prior to the arrival of the 'Europe' some £4 million would be spent on her to increase her freight capacity for the route.

The *Stena Europe* was originally built as the *Kronprinsessan Victoria* for the Gothenburg-Frederikshavn service of Sessan

During the refit of the **Koningin Beatrix** *in 2000 the former* **Stena Invicta** *covered on the route. She is seen here leaving Fishguard on her afternoon sailing to Ireland. (Mike O'Brian)*

The **Stena Lynx III** *is seen here arriving at Fishguard from Rosslare in August 2003. (Miles Cowsill)*

The **Stena Galloway** *is seen here at Rosslare during her final spell with the company covering for the refit of the* **Koningin Beatrix**. *(Gordon Hislip)*

Line. Shortly after her delivery Sessan Line was taken over by Stena Line and she was placed on the Gothenburg-Kiel route. In 1989 she was transferred to the Oslo-Frederikshavn service and renamed *Stena Saga*. Some five years' later, she was transferred to the Harwich-Hook of Holland service and placed under the British flag as the *Stena Europe*. Following the introduction of the HSS service between the UK and Holland, she once again returned to Scandinavia to operate for Stena Line's subsidiary company Lion Ferry between Karlskrona and Gdynia and was renamed *Lion Europe*. In 1998 she transferred back into Stena Line livery and was renamed *Stena Europe*.

The *Stena Europe* completed her operations in the Baltic on 25th January 2002 and was sent for refit and modifications. As part of her £4 million refit, all the cabins on deck 5 were removed to provide additional space for 61 more trailers. In addition to the removal of these cabins the shopping area and food and beverage outlets were refitted for her new role on the Fishguard-Rosslare route. She left Gothenburg on 6th March for Fishguard and arrived at the port for berthing trials three days' later. The next day she proceeded to Rosslare for berthing trials and then took up the service from there on 12th March commencing with the 09.00 sailing to Fishguard. This then

During the overhaul of the **Stena Europe** *in 2006 the* **Stena Seafarer** *covered for her absence on the route. (Gordon Hislip)*

The **Stena Lynx III** *maintains the Fishguard-Rosslare fast ferry service in tandem with the* **Stena Europe**. *(Gordon Hislip)*

allowed the *Koningin Beatrix* to sail to Poland for a short refit prior to entering service between Karlskrona and Gdynia as the *Stena Baltica*, where she still remains today.

The *Stena Europe* soon settled down into the *Koningin Beatrix*'s original roster operating in tandem with the fast craft operations of the *Stena Lynx III*.

The *Stena Lynx III* was due to complete her final season on the Fishguard-Rosslare service on 28th September. As agreed, she was then subsequently repainted, renamed *Elite* and returned to her owners, who had planned to sell her for further service in the Red Sea. In the event, the sale did not go through and in the early part of 2004 Stena Line acquired the former chartered vessel for the route at a cost of some £6.5 million, which also included a major overhaul as part of their investment. The vessel returned to the Fishguard link with her former name of *Stena Lynx III* but for 2004 appeared in a new livery for the company which included the Welsh dragon and the Irish shamrock. She re-opened the fast ferry route again on 8th April.

The **Stena Europe** *outward bound from Fishguard in September 2005. (Miles Cowsill)*

No replacement vessel was found for the absence of the *Stena Europe* for her refit and consequently the service between Fishguard and Rosslare was closed again between 31st January and 14th February 2004.

Sadly, during the summer of 2004 the *Stena Lynx III* had to be withdrawn from service with major crankshaft problems and as a result the fast ferry operation had to be suspended until 30th July.

It had been agreed within management that it was folly to close the route during the refit of the conventional ferry, and so for 2005 the company planned to transfer the *Stena Seafarer* from the Fleetwood-Larne route to cover for the 'Europe's' absence. In the event, the *Stena Seafarer* did not come south and the *Stena Europe*'s refit was deferred until May when the *Stena Caledonia* covered for the absence of the 'Europe' between 19th May and 12th June.

For 2006, the *Stena Seafarer* was transferred from the Fleetwood service to cover for the refit of the *Stena Europe* in January.

During August 2006, Stena Line celebrated the 100th Anniversary of the route with a series of high profile events on both sides of the St. George's Channel. The route remains an integral part of Stena Line's operations today and will continue to be a valuable link between the UK and Ireland as part of the transport infrastructure of the EU.

CALEDONIAN PRINCESS

This superb painting of the **Caledonian Princess** *by Robert Lloyd, marine artist, commissioned by Ferry Publications for the 100th anniversary of the Fishguard-Rosslare route, shows the vessel outward bound from Pembrokeshire to Ireland.*

CHAPTER FIVE

LINKING FISHGUARD WITH LONDON

by Richard Kirkman

The strategic advantage of the Pembrokeshire coast as an access point to Ireland was recognised by early railway developers.

The South Wales Railway Company (SWR) issued their prospectus in Summer 1844, with a strong focus on developing links with the South of Ireland via Fishguard supported by a significant proportion of Irish names amongst the provisional committee. The SWR was a front for the Great Western Railway (GWR) and Brunel was appointed Engineer of the proposed railway. The prospectus outlined plans for a line across the Severn Estuary, through Chepstow to Newport, and then via Cardiff, Swansea and Carmarthen to Fishguard, with a branch from Whitland to Pembroke Dock. The company sought capital of £2.5 million in £50 shares.

The majority of the route met with little opposition, but the section east of Newport proved contentious. The 1845 Act incorporated the SWR with a capital of £2.8m (of which the GWR contributed £600k). The Act also authorised a branch from near Clarbeston Road to Haverfordwest and construction work began in Summer 1846. Within a year progress could be measured along the length of the route to within seven miles of Fishguard. In December 1846 the railway was leased to the GWR, such an arrangement to commence when the line was complete from Gloucester to Fishguard.

Construction coincided with a dramatic peak in Parliamentary authorisation of new railway building in the UK. In 1841, 15 miles of new line had been approved; by 1846 this had risen to 4,541 miles in one year. This railway mania came to an abrupt end as the economy was hit by the repeal of the Corn Laws, the Irish potato famine and a dramatic rise in the cost of cotton from America. The resultant increase in the cost of imports put pressure on bullion reserves and availability of capital. In 1849, only 17 miles of new railway were authorised.

The SWR was not immune to the repercussions of this financial crisis, and the company sought to slow construction

An early view of Fishguard Harbour showing platforms 2 and 3. Today the extensive canopy has been removed and only one of these platforms is now used. (Martin Lewis collection)

A crowd gathers on the footbridge as the pairing of year-old GWR Flower class locomotives 4111 **Anemone** *and 4116* **Mignonette** *wait to double-head the morning special train to Paddington on 30th August 1909. Note the railings in the foreground. (Author's collection)*

progress on the new route, eventually electing to concentrate effort east of Swansea - where the greatest traffic potential lay. The Directors - perhaps mindful of the significant expense of constructing harbour facilities - sought to abandon the extension to Fishguard, as it became increasingly apparent that the Irish railways providing the reciprocal links to shipping services were unlikely to be built. The SWR and GWR eventually agreed that the line be built to Neyland Point rather than Fishguard. Construction work thereby ceased west of Clarbeston Junction - despite work having begun on some 7 miles of formation - and the line was opened in 1856. A steamship service to Waterford was inaugurated from the new harbour that Brunel built at Neyland.

The opening of a railway to Fishguard was left to more local interests.

The Narberth Road & Maenclochog Railway was constructed to serve the slate quarries at Rosebush in the Preseli Hills. It opened in 1876 and later formed part of a scheme to extend to Fishguard in conjunction with the Rosebush & Fishguard Railway. This latter company was incorporated in 1878 to build a 14-mile route from Rosebush to Goodwick. Although the two companies reached an arrangement in 1881, the scheme lapsed.

Powers were revived in 1884 by the North Pembroke & Fishguard Railway. Its route left the GWR west of Clynderwen and wound towards its destination via Maenclochog and Letterston. Construction began under powers granted to the Rosebush & Fishguard Railway, but major works did not begin until 1893.

Two Birmingham businessmen – Joseph Rowlands and John Cartland – realised the potential of the shorter sea route to Ireland via Fishguard and sought to raise the necessary capital to build a rail link, or to force the GWR to complete their route. In 1893, together with Irish interests, they incorporated the Fishguard Bay Railway and Pier Company with a capital of £120k, envisaging construction of a harbour and breakwater, together with a one-mile link to an extension of the North Pembrokeshire line. At the same time, the two businessmen financed the completion of the North Pembrokeshire line and this opened to Letterston in 1895.

The GWR had been happy to sit back and observe these local developments, but when the London & North Western Railway (L&NWR) was approached to help finance a new line from Clynderwen to Carmarthen they saw the threat that L&NWR access to Fishguard could bring to their Irish business. The L&NWR was committed to Irish services via Holyhead, and saw

With the growth of traffic on the Fishguard services to Cork, Rosslare and Waterford, the Fishguard Bay Hotel established an excellent service for travellers on the Great Western Railway. This picture shows an early view of the Hotel. (Martin Lewis collection)

The sheer scale of the earthworks required to create the port facilities at Fishguard is apparent in this period view of the new station. The immaculate condition of the rail infrastructure is clear as a rake of cattle wagons stands awaiting traffic from Ireland at the siding throat and **St. David** *lies alongside the quay. (National Museums & Galleries of Wales)*

few commercial opportunities that would be better served from Fishguard, so the request was declined. Undeterred, Rowlands and Cartland pressed ahead with their plans and developed them to incorporate a route into South Wales to attract coal traffic for export. Successive Acts of 1894 and 1895 saw the Waterford & Wexford Railway and the Rosslare Harbour Commission vested in the Fishguard Bay Railway and Pier Company, to form the Fishguard & Rosslare Railways and Harbours Company (F&RRHC).

The GWR was in expansive mood at the end of the 19th century. A reprise of the plans for Fishguard fitted well with the soon to be shortened journey times on the South Wales - London route. 1898 saw agreement reached with the F&RRHC and the Great Southern & Western Railway of Ireland (GSWR) to complete the 37 miles of railway necessary to link Waterford and Rosslare and the extension from the North Pembrokeshire line to Fishguard Harbour, to which the GWR contributed £250k. The agreement stipulated that the F&RRHC would complete the harbours and provide the steamers, with the GWR and GSWR operating the harbours and railways on each side of the Irish Sea. This left the residual anomaly of an Irish interest in a Welsh railway.

The North Pembrokeshire line extension to Goodwick opened on 1st July 1899. The latter was renamed Fishguard & Goodwick – acknowledging its closer proximity to the town - on 1st May 1904. A small engine shed with a 65 ft turntable opened here on 3rd August 1906.

Construction of the new facilities at Fishguard was to prove an epic undertaking, driven by the Chief Engineer of the GWR, James Inglis. Over 2 million tons of rock were progressively blasted from the cliff face to create 27 acres of land for the quay. The sound of blasting could be heard as far away as Newcastle Emlyn. Unsurprisingly this undertaking took longer than expected. Marine staff at New Milford expected to transfer to

The station canopy viewed from the south. The original canopy spanned all four platforms at Fishguard Harbour. (Martin Lewis collection)

Fishguard in 1902, but it was a further three years before the quay wall was completed and the station constructed.

The quay at Fishguard was over 1,000 ft in length and capable of handling three steamers simultaneously. The quay wall was constructed from some 4,900 concrete blocks, built on site and varying in size from 6 to 10 tons. Around six miles of sidings were built to serve the quay. Goods could be transhipped by nine 30-cwt electric cranes and a 21-ton crane for larger items and coaling of vessels. A gallery below passenger level allowed cattle to disembark unseen to a 650ft pen – capable of holding 1,000 head of cattle - for significant livestock trade was expected. An outbreak of foot and mouth disease in 1912 saw suspension of cattle movements for 11 months but led to substantial improvements in the facilities, including roofing and electric light.

The new station opened on 30th August 1906, with the overnight transfer of ships, trains and staff from New Milford. It

This view shows the loading siding for cargo and mail for the Cork, Rosslare and Waterford vessels. (Martin Lewis collection)

An overview of the station from the hillside to the south shows the extensive cattle pens on the landward side of the station and a splendid line-up of idle cranes grouped together. (National Museums & Galleries of Wales)

had two 789 ft island platforms served by four lines, and an overall roof. Ample waiting rooms and refreshment rooms were provided for all three classes. The functional style reflected its role as a transit point between rail and sea, with a subway and a movable bridge-platform permitting easy access to the steamers.

Such facilities provided substantial employment, the railway operations alone necessitating over 100 staff. It was estimated that between 25 and 30 coaling men would be required to refuel the steamers and up to 50 casual porters to assist with traffic.

The 'Wyncliff Hotel' was originally a private house which was purchased by the F&RRHC in 1894. Following takeover by the GWR in 1898, the hotel was renamed 'The Fishguard Bay Hotel' in 1906 and extended four years later. The sub-tropical hotel grounds included a croquet lawn and tennis court and guests could enjoy fishing on 7 miles of fishing rights on the Western Cleddau River. It continued to be operated as a railway hotel until 1951, when it was closed as part of a re-appraisal of hotel strategy following nationalisation; the freehold eventually passed from British Transport Hotels in 1967. The hotel is still trading.

Close to the hotel at Pen Cw Goodwick, the GWR built a garden village overlooking the bay to house the influx of port and railway workers. The company responded to the sensitivity of building on a prominent site by clustering houses on 13 separate sites; the whole development eventually comprised 112 properties. Prices ranged from £148 10s to £175. To support the community feel, the GWR also constructed a reading room and a library. A debating society, amateur dramatic society, bazaars and concerts were encouraged by the company. A wireless station was built alongside the village to communicate with the Rosslare vessels.

The GWR demonstrated its commitment from the opening of the new route on 30th August 1906, with a high speed service from Paddington departing at 08.45, calling intermediately at Newport, Cardiff and Landore (for Swansea) before arrival at Fishguard at 14.20. An evening connection was provided by a 20.45 departure from Paddington. The morning train called at Reading and the evening service at Swindon. Engines were changed at Cardiff en route and both trains featured restaurant car service. In 1907 the night services were enhanced by the introduction of new 70-foot First Class sleeping cars, reaching new heights in passenger comfort, but counter-balanced by a somewhat unattractive 02.15 arrival at Fishguard.

Passenger and freight traffic grew comfortably as the new route became established, helped by events such as the passage of Irish pilgrims to Lourdes for which special connecting trains were laid on to Folkestone.

However, this was not enough for the GWR. The circuitous single-line route of the NP&F was not compatible with main line running and, with an eye to getting a foothold in trans-Atlantic traffic, powers had been obtained in 1898 for a new line to be constructed over 10 miles from Clarbeston Road, through the 243-yard Spittal Tunnel to Letterston Junction and thence down a 1-in-50 gradient to the harbour site, thereby providing a more direct route to Fishguard. For a mile this route followed the alignment of the earlier abandoned scheme, with one of Brunel's original bridges finally completed some 60 years after it

The first **Mauretanian** *Special to leave Fishguard in 1909 was hauled by two 4-4-0 engines: No. 5402* **Halifax** *(City class) and No. 4108* **Gardenia** *(Flower class). It was necessary to use two engines to haul the heavy trains up the very steep bank at Manorowen. (Martin Lewis collection)*

was started. The Treffgarne Gorge proved a problematic obstacle for the GWR engineers, but the new line was built to a high specification. The junction with the Milford Haven line was laid in anticipation of high speed running, only the third junction on the GWR to be laid to this specification.

The GWR was notable for its pioneering efforts to promote its services. Southern Ireland: Its Lakes and Landscapes was published in Summer 1906 describing the scenic attractions in detail, but losing no opportunity to promote the benefits of the new Fishguard route, which would 'mark a new epoch in the history of travel in Southern Ireland'.

The GWR had long held ambitions to be a significant force in trans-Atlantic trade and great efforts were made to attract business to the new port. The importance of Fishguard lay in it being the closest UK call to New York. The main business was from Liverpool, but Plymouth and Southampton were growing in importance. The GWR had already developed traffic to Plymouth; now it saw an opportunity to steal business from arch rival the L&NWR. Trans-Atlantic liners already made brief calls in Ireland to drop off mail and passengers; if a similar stop could be made at Fishguard, substantial trade could be expected. The port lay 50 miles closer to New York than Plymouth and 100 miles closer than Liverpool. For a while Holyhead was seriously touted as an alternative intermediate call

A special train for the inaugural call of the RMS **Mauretania** *at Fishguard leaves for Cardiff and Paddington on 13th August 1909. (Martin Lewis collection)*

The dining saloon on the Ocean Express. The GWR spared no expense in promoting Cunard traffic. (National Museums & Galleries of Wales)

by the L&NWR, but local climatic conditions and the difficulties of enhancing facilities in an Admiralty port scuppered progress.

Booth Line were the first to call at Fishguard on 2nd April 1908 when the *Lanfranc* disembarked 21 passengers sailing from South America en route to Liverpool; Cunard Line became convinced of the port's potential a year later. There followed high profile calls by the *Mauretania* - the well-documented first visit on 30th August 1909 saw 880 bags of mail transferred to three tenders to feed three special services to Paddington. The mails took the first departure, and the two passenger trains enjoyed high speed runs to the capital in 4 hours 37 minutes and 4 hours 52 minutes, arriving well ahead of schedule and setting a new record of 5 days 3 hours 32 minutes for the journey from New York to London. Considerable effort was made by senior GWR management to ensure the success of this venture, with a high profile presence in the Harbour and the Company Chairman, Viscount Churchill, travelling from Queenstown on the vessel.

The trains typically comprised a luggage van, 8 First Class carriages, a restaurant car and a brake van. Ocean liner arrival times were unpredictable, so the special trains were not given specific paths in the timetable, relying instead on 'point to point'

An unidentified 'Flower' class loco heads away from Fishguard. (Pembrokeshire County Council)

timings from which signalmen could calculate arrival times, based on a telegraphed message 15 minutes before departure.

The twin shortcomings of Fishguard quickly became clear. The use of tenders to transfer mail and passengers was inconvenient and could not be accomplished in adverse weather conditions, forcing eastbound passengers to travel on to Liverpool: and the steeply-graded rail route out of the port required trains to be double-headed. The GWR responded in 1908 by obtaining powers to build an 'Ocean Quay' on the north side of the Harbour, and a new more easily graded 3 mile 53 chain alignment from Fishguard to Letterston, with two lengthy tunnels.

The most celebrated run occurred on 22nd December 1910 when five connecting trains left Fishguard and a special service chartered by the Daily Mail reached Paddington in 4 hours 31 minutes at an average speed of 57.8 mph. In March 1910 Cunard withdrew from Queenstown but this was not well received in Ireland. Later that year Blue Funnel Line included Fishguard on their Australian service and attempts were made to persuade White Star Line to call.

This route was very convenient for the substantial volume of traffic of visitors from America travelling to Europe. In conjunction with the South Eastern & Chatham Railway the GWR operated the 'Cunard Ocean Express Fishguard-Dover' direct from Fishguard to Dover on a seven-hour schedule.

Further along the route to Paddington, the opening of the Swansea District Lines on 14th July 1913 eased congestion and grade for trains passing Swansea - an 11-mile diversionary route, including two large viaducts and three tunnels - and a proposal soon followed for a similar scheme to bypass Llanelli. However, the First World War intervened and the works at Llanelli were abandoned.

Enthusiasm for further spending on the port appears to have waned, for it was difficult to justify continued investment for what were still only intermittent and intermediate calls for ocean liners. The more ambitious plans were cut back, and the political consequences of the capture of trans-Atlantic traffic from Ireland became clear when the Fishguard & Rosslare Railways and Harbours Bill was defeated in Parliament by a coalition of Irish and Labour interests.

On 16th June 1914 the ***Aquitania*** called on her return maiden voyage from New York and required five special trains to transfer over 600 passengers to London. Even larger numbers were carried on her next call, a month later. Sadly the outbreak of war brought a swift end to the trans-Atlantic trade, the tragic ***Lusitania*** being the last liner to visit Fishguard on 14th September 1914.

The celebrated and much photographed Mauretania boat trains wait to depart from Fishguard on 30th August 1909. Nos 5402 **Halifax** *and 4108* **Gardenia** *head the first train - a second departure stands in the adjacent platform. (Pembrokeshire County Council)*

'The Irish Express via Fishguard' is hauled by Class 4-4-0 No.3408 **Killarney** *en route from Paddington. (Martin Lewis collection)*

Opportunity still arose in 1915 with an approach to the GWR from the Anglo-Persian Oil Company, who were looking to build a refinery with nearby sea access. The negotiations came to naught, partly because the GWR felt that the traffic might interfere with the resumption of post-war trans-Atlantic traffic.

The wartime withdrawal of the day crossing to Rosslare saw the corresponding departure from Paddington transferred to Pembroke Dock and Neyland. After the war the evening departure time was standardised at 19.55. The 'Irish Mail via Fishguard' slipped two coaches at Stoke Gifford to form a late evening service to Bristol. After a call at Newport and engine changes at Cardiff and Swansea, the train arrived at Fishguard at 01.40. The return working left Fishguard at 03.55, with a banking engine provided to assist up the steep gradients out of the port. Further assistance was provided at Gowerton before calls at Swansea, Cardiff, Newport and Reading and an arrival at Paddington at 09.47.

The down train comprised 11 coaches, including the two slip coaches for Bristol, a sleeping car, a restaurant car, a First Class car, three Third Class cars and three brake vans, hauled by a 'Castle' class locomotive. The up service featured nine coaches without the slip workings.

The post-war recovery was hit by both the General Strike and the worsening political situation in Ireland, which did little to encourage the return of trans-Atlantic traffic. Growth at Southampton and decline at Liverpool only served to emphasise the geographical isolation of Fishguard. The GWR must have quickly realised how poor their investment was proving and, almost in desperation, halts were opened at Mathry (for St David's) and Jordanston in 1923 and Welsh Hook in 1924 to try and capture some additional local traffic.With the return of war in 1939 and the cut back in shipping services, boat trains were reduced to one working each way at 19.05 from Paddington and 06.05 from Fishguard and sleeper services were withdrawn,

An early view of Paddington Station as passengers embark on the special express to Fishguard. (Martin Lewis collection)

A view taken in May 1958 with the 0-6-0 pannier tank loco 8739 and one coach and van unit now forming the train service to London. How things have changed in 50 years from the glory of the opening of the port! (Martin Lewis collection)

Until recently Fishguard was connected during the peak season by an InterCity 125 HST service. Now passengers have to travel by Arriva Trains Wales to either Swansea or Cardiff to connect to the First Great Western service to London Paddington. This picture shows an HST unit at Whitland bound for Fishguard. **(Miles Cowsill)**

never to return.

From 1st October 1945 the 08.55 departure from Paddington had a Fishguard portion reinstated on Tuesdays, Thursdays and Saturdays, but evening passengers were required to leave at 18.55 on a train which ran through from Swansea to Fishguard only on Mondays, Wednesdays and Fridays. Arrival at Fishguard Harbour was at 01.15. The return journey on Tuesdays, Thursdays and Saturdays did not leave until 04.55 and despite reverting to the Swansea avoiding route, was not scheduled to arrive in Paddington until 11.40.

The drop in traffic after the Second World War resulted in a real threat to the survival of any passenger services in West Wales with the Beeching Report proposing the withdrawal of services west of Swansea. An immediate casualty was the withdrawal of cattle trains. The line from Clarbeston Junction to Fishguard was reduced to single track, and the four intermediate halts were closed on 6th April 1964. The engine shed at Fishguard & Goodwick closed and the Harbour station was reduced to one open platform and one spare.

Amidst the general depression in West Wales railway matters Fishguard Harbour provided grounds for optimism. With the conversion of the *St. David* to car carrier the daytime service from Paddington was re-instated in Summer 1964 for the first time in 50 years. An early motorail service from Kensington Olympia followed in 1965, but the growing volume of car traffic necessitated extensive rationalisation of the rail facilities at Fishguard Harbour. Just when things were looking up for rail services, cattle traffic from Waterford was lost in 1967 and the B&I business transferred to Swansea in 1968.

The Menai Bridge fire in 1970 saw a flurry of activity with container traffic transferred from Holyhead, but other business continued to decline. Freightliner services struggled on until the closure of the Waterford service in 1978. The motorail service from London was withdrawn in 1980.

In 2006 there are just two trains a day serving Fishguard. The port can be reached in 4 hours 26 minutes from Paddington, with the First Great Western departure at the traditional morning time of 08.45, albeit with a change of train (and train operator to Arriva Trains Wales) at Cardiff. The return daytime journey takes slightly longer at 4 hours 54 minutes, but connections from the overnight crossings are poorer, with the 01.50 from Fishguard Harbour requiring two changes of train and a 2 hours 17 minutes connection at Llanelli to reach Paddington at 08.59.

Few areas of Britain witnessed such a lengthy gestation between planning and construction of a railway. The ambitious plans to develop Fishguard were thwarted by a succession of external events and the anticipated potential was never realised. Paradoxically, the growth of ferry services has coincided with a decline in connecting rail services, now just a shadow of their former glories.

CHAPTER SIX

RAILS FROM ROSSLARE

by Bernard Share

FOUNDED IN 914 BY VIKING ENTREPRENEURS

Waterford is Ireland's oldest city. Sited on the long and narrow fjord-like estuary of the confluent Suir and Barrow rivers (hence the name: from the Scandianvian Vatnfjordur) it had been from its earliest days a significant transport centre. If the Irish name, Port Láirge, or the landing-place of the mythical Lairge, emphasises its maritime connections, the dawn of the railway age was to see it develop into an equally important locus of the internal transport system.

The Waterford and Passage Railway; the Waterford, Carlow & Dublin Junction Railway; the Waterford Free Bridge, Railway Bridge & Tramways; the Waterford, Lismore & Fermoy Railway; the Waterford Railways Junction & Tramways – all these undertakings, apart from including the name 'Waterford' in their titles, share another important element in common: none of them was ever built. The era of the railway mania in the middle and latter years of the 19th century was responsible, both in Ireland and elsewhere, for a plethora of schemes destined to fall victim to Parliamentary disapproval or commercial insolvency. As far as Ireland is concerned, a quick count reveals over 80, from the Armagh, Coleraine & Portrush Junction Railway to the Woodlawn, Mount Bellew & Mount Talbot Tramway, which were never to see the light of day. For a country of less than four million people still recovering from the devastation of the Great Famine that is a considerable total.

As for Waterford and its environs, the Cork & Waterford, incorporated as early as 1845 to link the two cities, failed to raise enough capital and stopped short at Youghal; before it, in 1826 at the very dawn of the railway age, the Limerick and Waterford Railway Company had received Parliamentary sanction, though again the scheme came to nothing. It was not until 1854 that Waterford was to emerge from this looking-glass

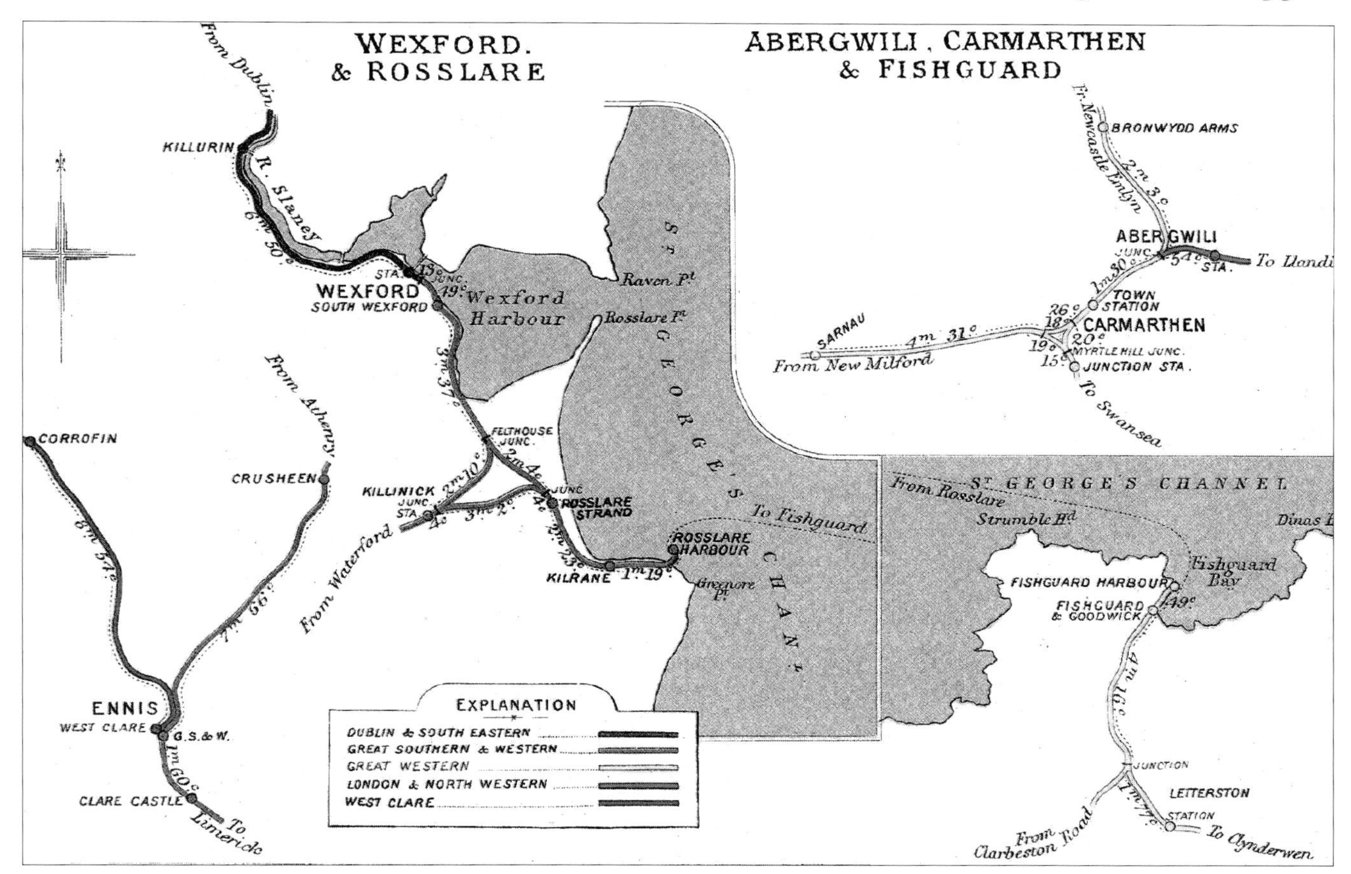

The 1914 Railway Clearing House map of Railway Junction Diagrams shows the rail links to both Rosslare and Fishguard Harbours.

The scene on 21st July 1906 with the service steamer alongside suitably dressed for the occasion of the official opening of Rosslare Harbour. The railway carriage to the right is the Royal Saloon (No. 351) built at Inchicore Works of the GSWR for the visit of King Edward VII and Queen Alexandra, and is now preserved in running order. (Courtesy of John F Hayes and John Power)

railway world, when the re-born Limerick and Waterford finally reached the city, to be followed in the same year by the last stretch of the Waterford & Kilkenny, linking it via the Great Southern & Western with the capital, Dublin. In this year Ireland as a whole could boast some 225 kilometres (190 miles) of railway carrying seven million passengers. Twenty years later the comparative figure stood at 3350 km (2,100 miles), destined to grow to a maximum of close to 8000 km (5,000 miles) in 1922. Waterford itself was, at its height, to boast three separate stations serving a complexity of railway undertakings, amongst them a comparative latecomer, the unmemorably named Fishguard & Rosslare Railways and Harbours Company – even the acronym, F&RRHC, failed to roll trippingly off the tongue.

The origins of this undertaking – which only ever possessed two locomotives and a handful of rolling stock, and that for a short period of four years – lie in the intense interest displayed by the Great Western Railway of England in the potential of the Irish Sea traffic. By the mid-1800s the London & North Western Railway, with its route via Holyhead to Dun Laoghaire (then known as Kingstown) held the bulk of the market. Holyhead had handled the Irish mail traffic, first privately and then under the aegis of the Post Office, since the 16th century. The GWR had envisaged a competing steamer service from Fishguard to Wexford, and was prepared to sponsor the construction of railways in Ireland as feeders to the new route. Famine in Ireland and a financial recession in Britain halted these plans, Paddington withdrawing from its Irish schemes before the projected lines had been built. Better times in the 1860s saw a renewal of its interest, however, and with Wexford Harbour revealed as likely to present serious problems due to silting, a decision was taken in Paddington to develop Rosslare, Co. Wexford, though at the time there was no harbour at all at the location, then known as Greenore. Another and more established Greenore, in Co. Louth, had, coincidentally, acquired its own Holyhead steamer service, again operated by the London & North Western, in May 1873.

To attempt to disentangle the complexities of early Irish railway history is no task for the faint-hearted, and one which will not be attempted here. Apart from the lines that were planned but never built there were those which, though

The River Barrow Bridge, Underbridge 140 and at 650 metres the longest bridge in Ireland. There are 15 spans including two swing sections for navigation and the girders were fabricated by the contractors, Arrols of Glasgow at their works. (Courtesy of Michael Barry)

The "Red Iron Bridge" as it is known locally carried the railway over the River Suir outside Waterford towards Mallow in Co. Cork where the line connected with the main Dublin-Cork line of the GSWR. (Courtesy of IRRS collection)

rejoicing in confident titles such as the Fermoy & Lismore Railways, never ran a train in their own right. This latter, financed almost entirely by the Duke of Devonshire, through whose Lismore estates it ran, was worked from its inauguration on 1st October 1872 by the Great Southern & Western as an extension of its branch from Mallow. Its operations were transferred to the Waterford, Dungarvan & Lismore Railway in 1893, only to revert to the GSWR when the latter took over both concerns in 1898, giving it access to Waterford and thus enabling it to play a key role in what will in future be referred to, as it was by its own Board and nearly everyone else, as the Fishguard Railway.

If all this sounds excessively complicated, it was to get worse, so much so that when in the late 1970s the Board of Córas Iompair Éireann (CIÉ), Ireland's national transport undertaking which had inherited the Irish end of the Fishguard Co, decided that it was an anachronism and that it would be better disposed of as a legal entity, the lawyers cautioned that the accumulation of relevant legislation and complex property rights since 1898 would probably involve not only an inordinate measure of time and expense but new legislation in both the Irish and British jurisdictions. For the fact is that, through all stages of successive ownership – GWR to British Railways to Stena Sealink on the British side; GSWR to Great Southern to CIÉ to Iarnród Éireann in Ireland – the Fishguard Co. remained nominally proprietors of both the sea crossing and the harbours at each end and the railway from Rosslare to Fermoy, though operating no vessels and owning no trains. The service, however, continued to function successfully, and it was thus decided, on the basis of 'if it ain't broke, don't fix it' to leave well enough alone.

The Company, with its maritime aims and euphonious title, was the creation not of the then established railway interests but of a Birmingham solicitor, Joseph Rowlands, who in the early 1890s recognised the potential of Fishguard as the terminus of a short sea route to Ireland. In 1895 his company was authorised to operate not less than one sailing daily between Fishguard and Rosslare, and he sought the support of both the GWR and the GSWR. The former, anxious to keep the predatory London & North Western well away from what it regarded as its fiefdom, opened negotiations with Rowlands in 1897 and with the Great Southern & Western the following year, resulting in the Act of 1898 authorising the new joint company to build lines from Rosslare Strand to Waterford and from Fermoy to Dunkettle on the GSWR's existing railway linking Youghal to Cork, thus ensuring through running to what is only partially sarcastically described in Ireland as 'the Southern Metropolis' or, if you are a Corkman, 'the real capital'. The GSWR was to operate these railways, and also to press the Corkmen to create a link between its terminus and the railway systems on the far side of the River Lee serving the then remote fastnesses of West Cork. Both this scheme and the proposed Fermoy-Dunkettle link were to be projects which the Fishguard Company were to live to regret.

The old Waterford North Station as built prior to the opening of the F&RRHC link. The main platforms and canopies continue to serve the modern railway but the structure was rebuilt in modern style during the 1960s. (Courtesy of IRRS collection)

The first meeting of the Board of the reconstituted Company was to occupy two days – the 8th and 9th of July 1898. At the third meeting, on 26th October at Paddington, where all meetings, with rare exceptions, have been held since, the Earl Cawdor, subsequently to be elevated to the position of First Lord of the Admiralty, was elected Chairman, his deputy, Joshua Pim, Chairman of the GSWR, representing that Company. Present were staff members from both railways, and the two Chief Engineers, Inglis, GWR, and Bayley, GSWR, were asked to report as to 'the best scheme for making connections across the River Lee with the Cork, Bandon & South Coast Railway and the Cork & Macroom Railway'. It was agreed that the existing railway linking Rosslare with Wexford, which had been opened in 1882, closed in 1894 because of poor receipts and opened again in 1894 when Rowlands' original Fishguard Co. had begun to work the line, should be placed under the control of the Great Southern & Western as from 1st November. The latter company was not too happy about this, as the line was well removed from the rest of their system, and said it would make a temporary arrangement with the Dublin, Wicklow and Wexford, which linked those centres, to operate it on its behalf. On the same date the GSWR was to take over the Waterford to Fermoy line still being operated by the Dungarvan and Lismore.

In December 1898 Kennett Bayley and Sir Benjamin Baker were given the task of building the railway from Rosslare to Waterford for a payment of 5 per cent commission on the sums falling due to the eventual contractors as well as on the permanent way materials. Tenders were invited in October of the following year for the construction of the line from Rosslare to a point near to the proposed Barrow Bridge, a distance of some 48 km (29 miles), the work to be completed by the end of June 1903. The new railway, as envisaged, faced major challenges in the matter of bridges across two major rivers – the Barrow, between Rosslare and Waterford, and the Suir, which had to be crossed at that city to connect with the line to Fermoy. If these were simple (or, in the event, not so simple) engineering problems, there was another which was to prove almost as demanding.

Joint lines, involving running powers shared by two or more railway companies, were (and are) uncommon in Ireland, but for the Fishguard Company to gain access to Waterford it would be necessary to share a very short length of track (about a quarter of a mile) with the Dublin, Wicklow & Wexford, subsequently to be renamed the Dublin & South Eastern

Restored J15 class steam locomotive No. 186 of the GSWR and now owned and operated by the Railway Preservation Society of Ireland. This once numerous class saw extensive service on the railways of South Wexford. (Courtesy of IRRS collection)

Railway, which was building an extension from its then terminus at New Ross into Waterford. Consultations were lengthy, disagreement emerging as to the precise location of the junction between the two lines. An otherwise insignificant thoroughfare known as Salvation Lane began to figure largely, Waterford Corporation entering the fray by refusing to approve plans for crossing it, a move which it considered would prejudice access to the North Wharf. In September 1901 the Dublin, Wicklow & Wexford complained that steps had not yet been taken by the Fishguard Co. to let the contract for the joint line to Messrs. Pearson & Son as agreed. Pearsons were building their New Ross-Waterford extension. Meanwhile work was proceeding on the main contract, which had been awarded to R. McAlpine & Sons of Glasgow, the lowest, at £144,435 3s 5d, of the five tenders received, the only Irish submission coming from Fisher & Lefanu of Kilkeel, Co. Down. By March 1902 there were three 'steam navvies' and three locomotives at work and almost 600 men employed, a figure that was predicted to rise to 1000 within two months with the addition of two more navvies and two locos.

Back in Paddington, Board meetings had regularly to turn their attention to the contingent questions of crossing the Lee and connecting Fermoy with Cork. In the matter of the former, the relevant Cork authorities were proving less than helpful. In February 1900 a letter to the Town Clerk of that city pointed out that though the Fishguard Co. had every desire to meet the views of the Corporation, no plan could be prepared of a suggested method of proceeding with the works until the site of the bridge was agreed. In proposing a meeting of engineers on both sides it sought clarity as to how the Corporation and the Harbour Commissioners proposed to co-operate with the Company. The Town Clerk responded that they were willing for the engineers to meet, 'provided it did not commit them in any way, even so far as the desirability of such a connection being made…' At this point Mr Hanbury, of the Treasury, stepped in, making it clear that the Government were very desirous of seeing the connection made and would endeavour, by conferring with the MPs for Cork City, to overcome the difficulties that had arisen.

The Government' s prime concern, of course, was not for the mobility of the people of Cork or indeed the commercial fortunes of the Fishguard Co. Their interest in Irish railways was predominantly strategic, seeing their development as being vital to the movement of troops between garrison towns, thus affording the means of a speedy response to any manifestations of disaffection. As far as the Fishguard Co. was concerned, however, the considerations were very largely financial. In July 1900 Hanbury informed them that 'unless the Board are able to assure the Treasury that arrangements have been made for providing for the execution of a scheme for connecting the two sides of the River they will be unable to agree to a further postponement of the repayment of the £93,000 due on the mortgage of the Waterford, Dungarvan & Lismore Railway.' This not inconsiderable sum, the outcome of the complex arrangements arising from the rationalisation of the route ownership between Waterford and Fermoy came, like Billy Bunter's postal order, to haunt the Company's affairs at every turn.

By the year 1901 Paddington were coming to realise that they simply lacked the resources to proceed with the other railway red herring, the Fermoy-Cork project. In reply to a letter from Maurice Healy, MP for Cork City, complaining that his constituents expected some public assurance on the matter, they claimed that it was intended to proceed with construction ' as soon as circumstances permit', citing the major expense they had incurred in the development of the Rosslare-Waterford line and the improvement of Rosslare Harbour. The Treasury was not so easily put off: in return for instructing the Board of Works to postpone the date for repayment of interest on the £93,000 it expected 'that the construction of the Cork and Fermoy direct line will proceed without interruption'.

At this juncture the Fishguard Co. had no choice but to put its cards on the table: in reply it stated that the line was not required and would not pay if it were built, 'and they therefore suggested that the Company should undertake to make the connections across the River Lee at Cork if the consent of the

In CIÉ days, a Rosslare-Dublin train makes its way cautiously along the quayside at Wexford. The line shares space with road traffic on this short section through the town. (Courtesy of IRRS collection)

local authorities could be obtained on condition that this Company be relieved of the obligation to construct the Fermoy line'. The statement was forwarded both to George Wyndham, the new Chief Secretary for Ireland, and Austen Chamberlain MP, shortly to become Chancellor of the Exchequer, but the Cork lobby remained unimpressed, the Town Clerk conveying the views both of the Corporation and the Harbour Commissioners that they could see no reason why the Company should be relieved of their legal obligation to construct the line. The Treasury also failed to concur with the abandonment proposal, but did agree to the further postponement of the repayment of the £93,000 until 1st October 1901. By the 24th of that month, however, it had still not been repaid and the Company sought a further postponement. This was by no means the end of the matter, with alternative schemes being promoted and rejected, but in the end the Fermoy-Cork line was never built, and the River Lee crossing was finally achieved in 1912 without any involvement by the Fishguard & Rosslare.

While Government were agonising over these matters work had been proceeding steadily on both the new railway and the extension and improvement of Rosslare Harbour. For the latter, the Company had sought the advice of 'a firm of eminent Marine Engineers', Messrs Coode, Son & Matthews of 9 Victoria Street, Westminster, but when they declined the invitation they turned to Captain F W Jarrad RN whose suggestions were adopted and tenders invited. The contract was awarded to Chas. Brand & Co, of Glasgow who commenced work in 1902. It specified a new viaduct connecting the pier with the mainland, a passenger platform, cattle platform, engine shed, rails and signalling, platform roof, goods shed, cranes and electric power, water supply, lighting and lighthouse. In June of the following year engineers Gordon and Otway, for the respective railway companies, reported that the work had been considerably delayed owing to the continued prevalence of heavy seas and rough winds which had held up the erection of the staging and interfered with the building in of the foundations and block setting. The 20-ton concrete blocks were being manufactured on site, and at this date 1024 had been produced. By the following February 2150 had been set of the 2540 made but there had been difficulties in pumping the required gravel to the blockmaking site on account of the bad winter weather. Six cylinders of the new viaduct were in place and finished to bed plate level. By May 1905 the east wall had been completed up to parapet level and the foundation core of the west wall carried out to meet the end wall which connected the two. When the new harbour opened the following year it was one of the most modern and efficient in Ireland or Britain.

In 1903 the Fishguard Co. suffered a double blow with the proximate deaths of the two General Managers – R G Colhoun of the GSWR and Sir Joseph Wilkinson of the GWR. In paying tribute, the Board recognised that 'both men had always taken a great interest in the Fishguard scheme and the latter was the author of it as far as the Great Western Company was concerned'. At this stage work was well advanced on the major engineering undertakings on the new line – the bridges over the Barrow and the Suir. There would be a cost overrun, Sir Benjamin Baker told his Board, borings having revealed that the soil in the beds of the two rivers would necessitate the piers being carried down deeper than was originally provided for – a perennial hazard of bridge-building in Ireland, as the

One of the famous J15 class of the GSWR, No. 116, starts her Mallow-bound train out of Waterford in the early part of the 20th century. Two of this class have been preserved - making them rare examples of locomotives which have worked through three centuries!. (Courtesy of IRRS collection)

The modern face of Iarnród Éireann, Irish Rail: A 2900 class four-car diesel multiple unit built by CAF of Spain now operates the bulk of services on the Rosslare route which from 2008 will benefit from a new fleet of specially constructed inter-city railcar sets offering even more 21st century comfort to the growing customer base using Irish railways. (Courtesy of Iarnród Éireann)

constructors of the pioneering Boyne Viaduct in 1855 had learnt to their cost. Of the ten tenders received for the Barrow works, that of Sir W. Arrol & Co. at £109,347 was accepted. By June 1904 all the piers except five had been sunk to their final depth, though Baker explained that progress had been slower than anticipated, but solely on account of the exceptional difficulties with the foundations. The Barrow Bridge was to become, at 650 metres (2131 ft), the longest in Ireland with 15 fixed spans and an electrically operated centre swing span to facilitate river traffic.

Arrol was also building the Suir Bridge and its approach railways, originally planned for a double track (the Barrow Bridge was, and is, single) but reduced to a single line with the agreement of the Dublin, Wicklow & Wexford Co., the latter company stipulating that their agreement was contingent upon the Fishguard Co. completing the joint line at the same time as their New Ross-Waterford line was constructed. The DW&W commenced the use of the joint line for goods on 15th February 1904 and for passengers on the 27th. Work progressed on the revised river crossing but in January 1906 the site was the scene of a serious accident when two men excavating inside a cylinder were killed by an unexplained explosion. Difficulties arose when the contractors working on a cutting encountered a soft, peaty material which gave rise to considerable slipping but at that stage it was hoped to complete the work by the end of July. In the event the bridge and approach railways were ready by the end of August for inspection by Colonel Von Donop on behalf of the Board of Trade who passed them, subject to some small requirements, for opening.

On Saturday 21st July Lord Abercorn, Lord Lieutenant of Ireland, travelled from Waterford to Rosslare to officiate at the formal inauguration of the Harbour and railways of the F&RRH Company, receiving a salute of 21 guns from the Coastguard as he passed over the Barrow Viaduct. The customary dinner, for some 400 guests, was hosted by Sir William Goulding, the GSWR Chairman. In 1906 there was still a 25-minute difference between Greenwich time and Dublin time, so that when regular services commenced on 30th August the 13-hour Paddington-Cork journey was slightly shorter – or longer – in one direction. Day and night sailings were scheduled from the beginning, with the former leaving London at 08.45, arriving Fishguard at 14.15, Rosslare at 17.10 and Cork at 21.20 – with the growing tourist trade in mind there was a connection at Mallow for Killarney. Thus a project which had its origins in an 1844 proposal by the GWR to extend the South Wales Railway to Fishguard Harbour had, 62 years later, finally borne fruit, and has flourished ever since.

CHAPTER SEVEN

THE FISHGUARD & ROSSLARE RAILWAYS AND HARBOURS COMPANY

by Gareth Williams

The ports of Fishguard and Rosslare are owned by the Fishguard & Rosslare Railways & Harbours Company (the Fishguard Company), and the joint owners of the Fishguard Company are Stena Line Ports Limited and Irish Rail (CIE).

The strong historical link between them all dates back to the late 19th century, when it was decided that a railway and pier should be built and maintained at Fishguard. In order to proceed with the proposal, legislation was necessary, hence the Fishguard Bay Railway and Pier Act 1893 which incorporated the creation of the Fishguard Company.

As a statutory company, the Fishguard Company is governed by its own Acts of Parliament (of which there were no less than nine between 1893 and 1914) and is not subject to the Companies Acts and other similar legislation.

By virtue of the Fishguard and Rosslare Railways and Harbours Act 1894, the Fishguard Company then took over the bankrupt Rosslare Railway and Harbour undertaking. Further Acts, in 1898 and 1899, brought the Company into the ownership of two railways – the Great Western Railway Company of England and the Great Southern & Western Railway Company of Ireland.

The Act of 1898 was particularly significant, stating:

"The Fishguard Company is authorised to construct a harbour in Fishguard Bay with a railway from the harbour to Goodwick, where it will be connected with the system of the North Pembrokeshire & Fishguard Railway Company. The Fishguard Company is also authorised to own and work steamers between Fishguard and, amongst other places, the harbour of Rosslare."

On the Irish side, the Act stipulated that:

"The Fishguard Company, under statutory powers, are the owners of the harbour at Rosslare and the railway from Rosslare to Wexford, where it is connected with the system of the Dublin, Wicklow & Wexford Railway Company."

This rail link from Wexford to Rosslare was opened in 1882 and operated by the Dublin, Wicklow & Wexford Railway – but

The Current Board Directors of the pictured at the 111th AGM in February 2006. Left to Right: Standing: Michael Murphy, Richard O'Farrell (Deputy Chairman), Ian Jamieson, Vic Goodwin. Seated: Les Stracey, Gareth Williams (Chairman), John Keenan. (Stena Line)

The **St. David** *(II) pictured at Fishguard shortly after entering service on the route. (National Museums & Galleries of Wales)*

The Fishguard and Rosslare Railways and Harbours Company.
GUARANTEED PREFERENCE STOCK.
No. 328 £ 10,000
This is to Certify that The Manitoba & North West Land Corporation Limited of 1 Queen Victoria Street, London E.C. are the Registered Proprietors of Ten Thousand Pounds of Guaranteed Preference Stock in this Company issued under and subject to the provisions of the Fishguard & Rosslare Railways & Harbours Acts 1898 to 1903, and bearing interest during construction at the rate of 3 per cent per annum, and from the inauguration of the through service at the rate of 3½ per cent per annum in perpetuity.
Dated 28th July 1904
Registered Folio 435 Secretary.
This Certificate must be surrendered before any Deed of Transfer whether for the whole or any portion of the Stock can be registered or a new Certificate issued in exchange.

it was never profitable, the service ceasing in 1889. It resumed in 1894, when the Fishguard Company became the line's new owners, until the Great Southern & Western Railway subsequently took it over.

Management of the Welsh and Irish portions of the Fishguard Company's undertaking was delegated to these railway companies respectively by an Agreement in 1898, which is scheduled to the 1899 Act.

Stena Line Ports Limited is the successor to the Great Western Railway Company, owning 50% of the issued ordinary shares. Irish Railways, a subsidiary of CIE, are the successors of the Great Southern & Western Railway Company of Ireland, owning the other 50%.

The initial formation of the Fishguard Company in the early 1890s owes much to the foresight of a Birmingham solicitor, Joseph Rowlands, who saw the potential in a short sea route from Fishguard. He had no trouble interesting the GWR in his scheme, which dovetailed perfectly with their desire to improve links with Ireland.

At the turn of the 19th century, the whole of Ireland was within Great Britain. Accordingly, statutes were equally applicable in Ireland to the extent that Irish interests were involved. When the Irish Republic gained independence, existing statutes of the Westminster Parliament which affected Ireland, and which were not specifically repealed, remained in force as Irish Acts of Parliament.

The constitution of the Fishguard Company, being statutory, can only be changed with the authority of Parliament. Since both English and Irish interests are involved, the authority of both the UK and Irish Parliaments is likely to be required. Therefore, it has been considered impractical to initiate any change through legislation, such as giving the Fishguard Company increased powers to raise capital.

Under the statutory Agreements

A 1960s view of the **St. Andrew** *going astern at Fishguard. Note the funnel markings in this picture of the Fishguard & Rosslare Railways and Harbours Company. (National Museums & Galleries of Wales)*

which delegate the management of the respective port undertakings, Stena Line and Irish Railways retain all the receipts and bear all the expenses relating to Fishguard and Rosslare respectively. Also, each is responsible for servicing the capital raised for its respective ports.

There is still some publicly-held non-voting preference stock in the Fishguard Company. CIE, through its subsidiary Iarnrod Eireann (Irish Rail), is responsible for funding the interest on this stock, which was all raised for the Irish side of the undertaking. Stena Line Ports Limited, along with CIE, is joint guarantor of the publicly-held stock, and the guarantee is still backed by the British Railways Board.

THE FISHGUARD COMPANY'S CURRENT BOARD

This consists of seven directors – four nominated by Stena Line Ports Limited and three by Iarnrod Eireann (CIE):

Gareth Williams, Chairman: nominated by Stena Line
Richard O'Farrell, Deputy Chairman: nominated by CIE
Leslie Stracey, Company Secretary: nominated by Stena Line
Vic Goodwin: nominated by Stena Line
Ian Jamieson: nominated by Stena Line
Michael Murphy: nominated by CIE
John Keenan: nominated by CIE

Some of the earliest directors (1908) included such distinguished names as Viscount Churchill G.C.V.O. (Chairman), Sir William J.Goulding (Deputy Chairman) and Lord Barrymore of Queenstown.

THE RELEVANT ACTS OF PARLIAMENT

Fishguard Bay Railway and Pier Act 1893
Fishguard and Rosslare Railways and Harbours Act 1894
Fishguard and Rosslare Railways and Harbours (Steam Vessels) Act 1895
Fishguard and Rosslare Railways and Harbours Act 1898
Fishguard and Rosslare Railways and Harbours Act 1899
Fishguard and Rosslare Railways and Harbours Act 1900
Fishguard and Rosslare Railways and Harbours Act 1903
Fishguard and Rosslare Railways and Harbours Act 1908
Fishguard and Rosslare Railways and Harbours Act 1914

CHAPTER EIGHT

THE 54-MILE LINK - A MASTER'S VIEW

by Captain David Williams

Having served continuously on this route since 1975 I have witnessed many changes but the one aspect that has not changed at all is the whole reason for our being here, and that is to safely convey passengers, cars and freight vehicles from Wales to the Republic of Ireland and vice versa.

When I joined the Company it was the Shipping and International Services Division of British Rail and there were three ships based at Fishguard. One of these operated a thrice weekly container service to Waterford whilst the other two ships operated on the Fishguard to Rosslare service, one carrying passengers and cars and the other a dedicated freight ship. Upon the closure of the Waterford service in 1978 the Company concentrated all of its efforts on the Rosslare service and even in this relatively short period of time, many changes have been introduced as travelling trends have changed. Whereas we once had dedicated passenger ships with fairly limited space for the carriage of cars, travel trends have changed such that the car passenger is now our primary market. Ships have also grown in size and since 1979 this route has been served by only one multi purpose ship which has been able to combine the carrying of passengers, cars and freight vehicles whilst maintaining a regular schedule throughout the year with two sailings in each direction on every day except for Christmas Day and Boxing Day. There have also been changes of ownership when the Government sold the Company into the private ownership of Sea Containers who then sold it into the present ownership of Stena Line, and all of these changes have seen new and upgraded tonnage added to the route along with new ideas which have all helped to keep the service viable.

The role of a ship's Master has also changed over the years. Apart from the basic skills of seafaring which are of paramount importance, there are many other aspects to the job which have to be taken into consideration and prioritised if necessary. As we now operate on a live-aboard basis, the Master's duties are divided between the Master and the Mate/Master who takes over whilst the Master has his statutory rest period. My day officially begins at 08.00. with the ship berthed at Rosslare and loading passengers and cargo for the scheduled 09.00. sailing to Fishguard. After having been briefed by the Mate/Master about the two previous sailings, it's off up to the bridge to prepare for the next voyage. This entails reading the daily weather forecast which now arrives by e-mail from Aberdeen Met Office, signing the Change of Master form in the Official Log Book to say that I have now taken over command, carrying out some pre-sailing checks along with the Mate/Master, informing the engine room how loading is proceeding and, when loading is complete and

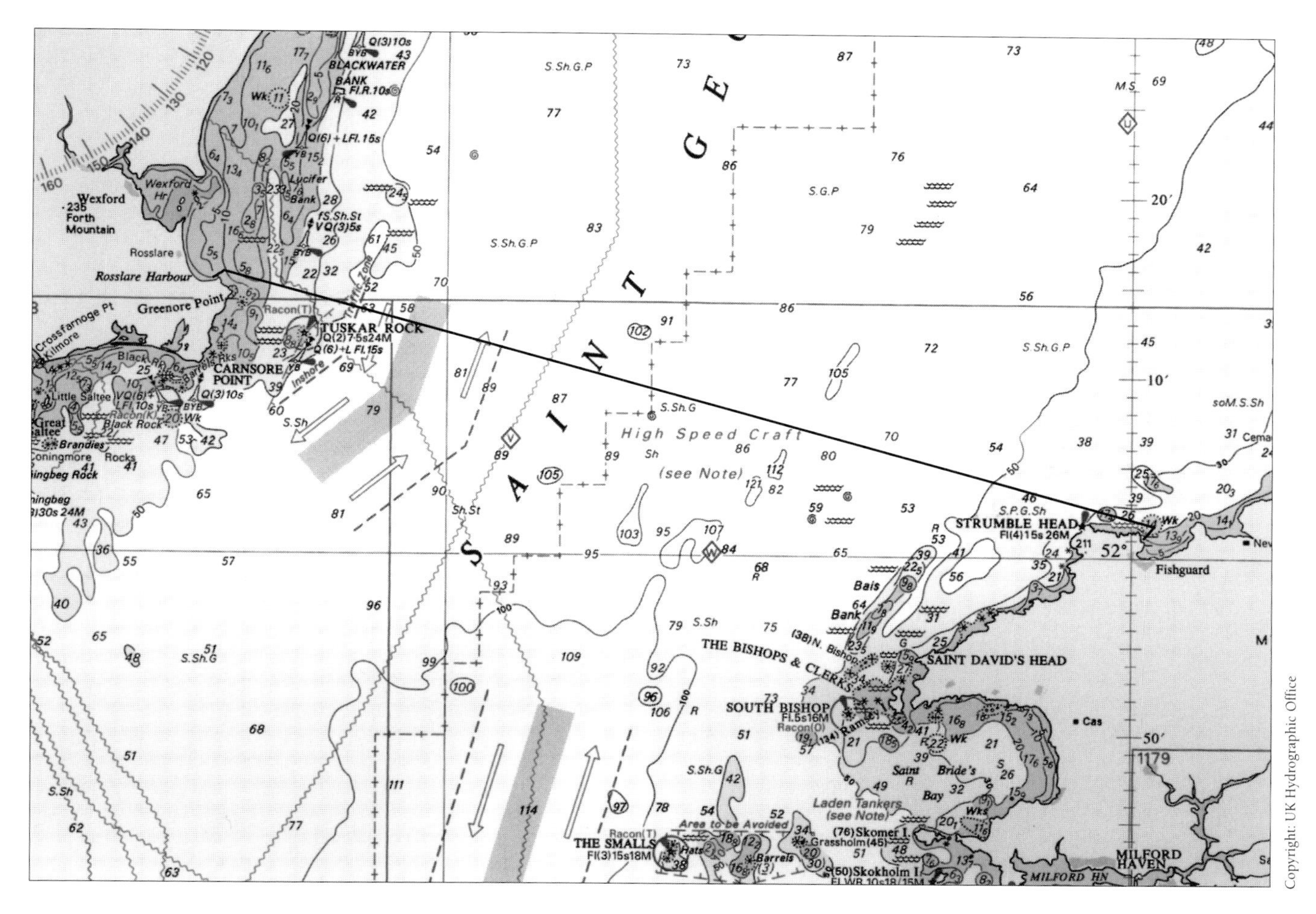

the stability has been checked, checking that all watertight doors, bow and stern doors are shut. After having been granted permission to sail from Rosslare Port Control, I ask the engineers to start the engines and it's off for a 3 hour 30 minute passage to Fishguard.

The first part of the passage takes us down a buoyed channel through the sandbanks off Rosslare until we pass our last point of land on the south east coast of Ireland which is Tuskar Rock lighthouse. The lighthouse which was manned until 1993 is now unmanned like all the other lighthouses which are serviced and maintained by Irish Lights and in fact achieved notoriety some years ago when it was used in a television commercial for being painted with Sandtex. After passing Tuskar Rock on our starboard side we have an open sea passage across St George's Channel for 43 miles until we pass our next major landmark which is Strumble Head lighthouse situated on the north Pembrokeshire coastline approximately 5 miles from Fishguard Harbour. It is during this 43 miles of open sea passage when the bridge is manned by the Officer of the Watch and a lookout that I get the time to attend to other important matters that arise. These include a meeting with the Chief Engineer to discuss any problems that may have arisen in the engine room, attending to an increasing amount of paperwork which has been brought about by any new legislation that has been introduced, liaising with the On Board Services Manager regarding the hotel department and chairing a weekly Heads of Department meeting.

As we now have an onboard ship management system, all of the stores and equipment required to operate the ship are sourced and ordered from on board and so a very watchful eye has to be kept on the budget otherwise some explaining will have to be done at a later date! Before too long my telephone rings to let me know we are not far away from Strumble Head and it's time for me to go to the bridge again for the last part of the passage. The coastline along north Pembrokeshire where we pass the site of the last invasion of Britain in 1797 and the approaches to Fishguard Harbour are at times quite breathtaking, especially when the abundant amount of heather and gorse is in full bloom after a long winter, and after rounding the breakwater and approaching the berth we moor bow to the ramp, open the doors, ship the gangway, discharge all our passengers, cars and freight and get the ship cleaned up and ready for loading for our return journey to Rosslare.

Having been born and raised at Fishguard I feel both proud and privileged to have spent the greater part of my career working on the Fishguard to Rosslare route and hope to see it continuing to prosper for many more years to come.

CHAPTER NINE

THE OTHER FISHGUARD ROUTES

by Miles Cowsill

FISHGUARD - WATERFORD

The link to Waterford opened originally in 1850 from Milford. When the port of Fishguard was opened in 1906, the *Great Western* and the *Great Southern* were transferred to the North Pembrokeshire port. Even at the time the Waterford service was considered to be the less superior operation to Rosslare. Both the *Great Western* (I) and the *Great Southern* had no great speed, only boasting 16 knots, but this was quite sufficient for the route with its long turn rounds. Saloon passengers were accommodated amidships while steerage travellers were aft.

In 1933, the *Great Western* (I) was replaced by a new vessel of the same name, built at the yard of Cammell Laird. She could only do 14 knots, but again this speed was sufficient. Her passenger accommodation for 450 passengers was in two classes and she was well appointed for the day, but in the main she was principally a cargo and cattle vessel. The service until the war was a night only service, carrying only small numbers of passengers compared to the Fishguard-Rosslare link.

When the Second World War broke out, the link was kept open on a spasmodic basis. The *Great Western* (II) for the greater part of the war served at Fishguard, with only a short break in April 1944 when she served as a troopship.

After the war, the service continued its pre-war pattern until June 1959, when it was announced that passengers would no longer be carried on the route. During the overhaul periods of the *Great Western* (II) until the late-Fifties, a number of vessels were commissioned to take her place, including the elegant *Princess Maud*, *Slieve Donard*, *Slieve Bearnagh* and the *Slieve Bawn*.

Following the decision not to take passengers on the service any longer, the *Great Western* (II) was re-fitted to carry more livestock and cargo. She was to maintain the Waterford service for a further six years until she was withdrawn from operations.

The gradual run-down of the Waterford service in the early-Sixties was of great concern amongst the townspeople of the

The **Great Southern** *is pictured here at Fishguard pending her sailing to Waterford. She was to remain an integral part of the route until she was replaced in 1934. (Martin Lewis collection)*

Irish port. In November 1964 a resolution was drawn up by the Council of Trade Unions urging the Board of British Rail to provide a replacement vessel for the *Great Western*. In the following February a law advisor to the Waterford Town Council maintained that BR were under a statutory obligation to maintain a daily cargo and passenger service, from an Act dating back to 1898, and that the termination of the passenger service in 1959 had been the result of a 'Gentlemen's Agreement', between British Rail and the Waterford authorities. At one stage there were high hopes that the townspeople would win their case, but in the end, following the decision of British Rail and the CIE in Ireland to invest in a new linkspan both at Fishguard and Rosslare, the people of the town knew they had lost their battle. The new facilities on the rival link would allow livestock to be driven by lorries on board the ships, thereby cutting down loading times. The introduction of this new and faster type of loading would make the Waterford service far less attractive for traders.

Following the *Great Western* being withdrawn from service at the end of 1966, she was replaced by the chartered container vessel *Eden Fisher*. Two years later, the *Harrogate* was transferred to the route in place of the chartered cargo vessel. In 1971, the *Container Enterprise* was moved from Heysham to operate the link three times a week in each direction, and some two years later she too was replaced by the longer *Isle of Ely*, which could carry 62 tons more than the previous vessel.

Loadings on the route continued to be steady. There was also to be a positive report on the future of the service published by the Welsh Council in September 1973. However, a month later the crane drivers at Waterford went on strike for a month. Traffic was immediately transferred to Rosslare, and this strike was to mark the long-term downfall of the route. Meanwhile, in November a new crane at Fishguard was built to enable the Waterford vessel to handle heavier cargoes.

In 1976, the *Container Venturer* replaced the ***Isle of Ely*** on the link. During the same year British Rail claimed that the Waterford service was now losing something in the region of £300,000 per year and that they would like to close the route. The unions on both sides of the St. George's Channel claimed

A view of the **Great Western** *(II) at Fishguard as cargo-only vessel. (Ferry Publications Library)*

In 1933 the **Great Western** *(II) was built by Cammell Laird for the Waterford service. The vessel is pictured here at Fishguard on her day layover at the port during her period as a passenger and cargo ship. (National Museums & Galleries of Wales)*

The City of Cork Steam Packet Co. vessel **Classic** *entered service on the Fishguard-Cork service in 1919. (Martin Lewis collection)*

The **Innisfallen** *(III) was built in 1948 and was slightly bigger than her predecessor. (Martin Lewis collection)*

that the company had failed to invest in the operation. However, the operation could not close overnight, as British Rail were under a statutory obligation to keep it open. During April, the Seamen's Union were lobbying politicians in both Ireland and Britain to save the route. By the end of the year the Labour Party were claiming that the route had been mis-managed and that it could be made to pay.

The new crane built at Fishguard collapsed across the deck of the *Container Venturer* on 2nd February 1977, while she was loading for Waterford. Traffic had to be transferred to Rosslare as a result of this incident, until repairs were completed.

A Committee of Enquiry was set up in 1977 to look into the future of the service. It was announced on 21st October that the Waterford service should be closed, as it was unprofitable with the Fishguard-Rosslare link so close at hand. On the same day, British Rail applied for the closure of the route as from March of the next year. The service closed on 19th March 1978, ending nearly 200 years of traffic between Pembrokeshire and Waterford. Following the route closing traffic was transferred to the drive-on vessel *Avalon* on the Rosslare service and to the container service at Holyhead.

THE CORK SERVICE

The link between Milford Haven, Pembrokeshire and Cork started back in 1857 with the steamer *Pacific* of the London-based company of Ford & Jackson. In 1871 the GWR obtained Parliamentary powers to operate their service, and as a result the railway company took over the established service to Cork.

By 1896, the City of Cork Steam Packet Co. were operating the link and the first vessel to carry the name *Innisfallen* had been built. By 1903, the *Inniscarra* was operating the service, following the *Innisfallen* being transferred to the Cork-Liverpool route. In 1906 the route moved to Fishguard where it was to

The City of Cork Steam Packet Company's vessel **Inniscarra** *takes on her cargo at the port of Fishguard prior to her evening departure to Cork. (Martin Lewis collection)*

This wonderful view taken from the hill overlooking the Harbour takes in the **Inniscarra**, *the original* **Great Western** *(I) and one of the 'Saint' class vessels on the Rosslare route. (Martin Lewis collection)*

stay until 1968. The *Inniscarra* was lost during the First World War and the Coast Lines vessel *Kenmare* was used to maintain the link until the the second *Innisfallen* was introduced on the route. The new vessel attracted increasing numbers to the route, which was advertised as '*The Innisfallen Way*'. The service operated ex-Cork on Mondays, Wednesdays and Fridays at 18.00 with arrival at Fishguard at 02.00 the following morning for the train service to London. Meanwhile sailings from Fishguard were on Tuesdays, Thursdays and Saturdays at midnight with arrival at Cork early in the morning.

The *Kenmare* took over the route again in 1940 and was eventually replaced by the newly-built *Innisfallen* (III) in 1948. She remained on the Cork route until 1968, prior to the service moving to Swansea.

The **Innisfallen** *(II) was built for the Cork service in 1931 by Harland & Wolff. (Martin Lewis collection)*

During the late-Sixties, B&I decided that they wanted a port of their own, and they also considered that Swansea would in the long term be a better port than Fishguard for Cork, once the M4 motorway reached the city from London. A new purpose-built vessel was constructed for the route and a new terminal at Swansea for the nine-hour link between Wales and Ireland. The modern looking *Innisfallen* (IV) built in Cork was modelled on the earlier *Munster* design built for company's Dublin-Liverpool service. The new ferry was built with a service speed of 21 knots, so she could maintain schedules for the route especially during bad weather. The new *Innisfallen* was in stark contrast to the vessel she replaced on the Fishguard service, with very modern lines and drive-on facilities for 245 cars. In 1978 the route moved back to Pembrokeshire to the port of Pembroke Dock; in the event it closed in 1983 following heavy losses.

FLEET LIST

compiled by Dick Clague

NAME	BUILT	BUILDER	FISHGUARD – ROSSLARE SERVICE DATES	NOTES
St. George	1906	Cammell Laird, Birkenhead	1906 – 1913	*sold to CPR 1913 – requisitioned 1917 – sold to Great Eastern Rly 1919 – scrapped 1929*
St Patrick	1906	John Brown, Clydebank	1906 – 1929	*scrapped after fire at Fishguard in 1929*
St David	1906	John Brown, Clydebank	1906 – 1932	*re-named Rosslare 1932 – sold for scrap 1933*
Mercury	1892	Robert Napier, Glasgow	1906	*cargo*
Pembroke	1880	Laird Bros, Birkenhead	1906 – 1925	*cargo only from 1916 – scrapped 1925*
St Andrew	1908	John Brown, Clydebank	1908 – 1932	*re-named Fishguard 1930 – sold for scrap 1933*
Great Southern	1902	Laird Bros, Birkenhead	1914	*wartime – scrapped 1934*
Great Western	1902	Laird Bros, Birkenhead	1914	*wartime – re-named G.W.R 20 (1933) – scrapped 1934*
Duke of Connacht	1902	John Brown, Clydebank	1914	*wartime - owned by London & North West Rlwy*
Dewsbury	1910	Earle, Hull	1915	*cargo*
St Patrick [II]	1930	A Stephen & Sons, Linthouse	1930 – 1941	*bombed & sank on F-R service*
St Andrew [II]	1932	Cammell Laird, Birkenhead	1932 – 1966	*scrapped 1967*
St David [II]	1932	Cammell Laird, Birkenhead	1932 – 1944	*sunk Anzio 1944 whilst serving as hospital ship*
St David [III]	1947	Cammell Laird, Birkenhead	1948 – 1969	*re-named Holyhead – sold to Greek owners 1971 – broken up 1979*
St Patrick [III]	1948	Cammell Laird, Birkenhead	1948 – 49	*transferred to English Channel – sold to Greece 1972 – re-named Thermopylae*
Slieve Donard [II]	1960	Ailsa, Troon	1966	*cargo vessel*
Duke of Rothesay [II]	1956	Wm. Denny, Dumbarton	1967 – 72/73/74	*scrapped 1975*
Caledonian Princess	1961	Wm. Denny, Dumbarton	1969 – 1975	*in use as a leisure centre in Gateshead since 1982*
Holyhead Ferry I	1965	Hawthorn, Leslie, Hebburn	1973 refit cover	*re-named Earl Leofric 1976 – scrapped 1981*
Neckartal	1970	Kroegerwerft Rendsburg	1973 charter in	*re-named Schiaffino in 1974 and Alba in 1991*

Following the disposal of the **St. George** *by the GWR her next couple of years of service were to take in operations in Canada in Newfoundland. She was later to be employed back in European waters in 1919. (Maritime Museum of the Atlantic)*

The **Stena Baltica** *(ex* **Koningin Beatrix***) arrives at Gdynia following her conversion and rebuilding in 2005. (Henk van der Lugt)*

The **St. David** *(II)leaving Birkenhead on her delivery voyage to Fishguard. (Willamson Art Gallery & Museum)*

The vessel that changed everything at Fishguard still goes strong today as the **Moby Vincent** (*ex* **Stena Normandica**). *She is seen here with her distinctive whale and livery of Moby Lines. (FotoFlite)*

The **Stena Europe** *entered service on the Irish Sea in March 2002. She is seen here at Harwich during her days on the Dutch service. (Miles Cowsill)*

NAME	BUILT	BUILDER	FISHGUARD – ROSSLARE SERVICE DATES	NOTES
Preseli	1970	Kroegerwerft Rendsburg	1974 charter in	*ex Isartal - later Pointer then Sea Malta's Zebbug in service 2005*
Duke of Lancaster [III]	1956	Harland & Wolff, Belfast	1975 & 1977	*cover until arrival of Avalon*
Avalon	1963	A Stephen & Sons, Linthouse	1975 – 77 – 79	*scrapped in Pakistan 1981*
Dover	1965	Swan Hunter, Wallsend	1976	*re-named Earl Siward 1971 - sold to Cyprus/re-named Sol Express 1982*
Anderida	1971	Trosvik Verksted, Brevik, Norway	1977	*sold to Greece 1981 and re-named Truck Trader*
Lord Warden	1952	Wm. Denny, Dumbarton	1978	*summer peak only – w/drawn 1979 – broken up as Al Zaher 1981*
Stena Nordica [II]	1974	Brodogradiliste,Trogir, Yugoslavia	1978 & 1980	*berthing trials 14/9/78 - relief - 1980 see Stena Londoner*
Stena Normandica	1974	Rickmers, Bremerhaven, Germany	1979 – 1985	*see St Brendan*
St Christopher	1981	Harland & Wolff, Belfast	1981 refit cover	*re-named Stena Antrim 1991 – Ibn Batouta (Limadet) 1998*
St Columba	1976	Aalborg Verft, Denmark	1982 refit cover	*Stena Hibernia 1991 / Stena Adventurer 1996 / Express Aphrodite 1997*
St David [IV]	1981	Harland & Wolff, Belfast	1983/7 refit cover	*see Stena Caledonia*
St Anselm	1980	Harland & Wolff, Belfast	1983 only	*2 day breakdown cover end March – see Stena Cambria*
Hengist	1972	AMNF Brest, France	1985	*breakdown cover – re-named Apollo Express 1987 - re-named Agios Georgios 2005*
St Brendan	1974	Rickmers, Bremerhaven, Germany	1985 – 1990	*ex Stena Normandica – later Moby Vincent - in service 2005*
Prins Philippe	1973	Temse, Belgium	1986	*3 week charter*
Innisfallen	1969	Verolme, Cork	1986 only	*later Derin Deniz - broken up 2004*
Vortigern	1969	Swan Hunter, Wallsend	1986/7 refit cover	*re-named Milos Express 1988 – Nissos Lemnos 2003 – broken up 2005*
Senlac	1973	Brest, France	1986	*summer peak only – Apollo Express I 1987 – Express Apollon 1995*
Darnia	1977	Osterreichische Schiffswerften, Linz, Austria	1988	*breakdown cover – built as Stena Topper. Sold to Sweden 1991*
Stena Sailer	1975	Verolme, Cork	1988	*St Cybi 1988 - laid up in Greece 2000 as Theseus*

Two old favourites of the Sealink fleet and of the Fishguard route at the end of their careers. The **Caledonian Princess** *and the* **Maid of Kent** *laid up at Newhaven. (Miles Cowsill)*

CALEDONIAN PRINCESS

Today the **Felicity** *is owned by Polferries and operates between Sweden and Poland as the* **Scandinavia**. *She is pictured here arriving at the port of Nynashamn. (Mike Louagie)*

During 2000 the **Stena Invicta** *was used for relief on the Fishguard-Rosslare route. Today she is employed with Stena Line as the* **Stena Nautica** *operating between Varberg and Grenaa. (Miles Cowsill)*

NAME	BUILT	BUILDER	FISHGUARD – ROSSLARE SERVICE DATES	NOTES
Earl Harold	1971	CNV - Venice	1988 refit cover	*ex Ailsa Princess – sold to Sri Lanka for further service 2005*
Cambridge Ferry	1963	Hawthorn Leslie, Hebburn-on-Tyne	1988 – 91	*freight back-up – Ita Uno 1992 – Sirio*
Felicity later Stena Felicity	1980	Landskrona, Sweden	1990 – 97	***re-named** Visby 1998 – Visborg 2002 – in service 2005 as Scandinavia (Polferries)*
Horsa	1972	Brest, France	September 1990	*12 hour breakdown cover 4.9.90*
Stena Cambria	1980	Harland & Wolff, Belfast	1990/92/98 17.11.90 – 8.12.90	*ex St Anselm – re-named Isla de Botafoc 1999 in service 2005*
Norrona	1973	Nobiskrug, Rendsburg	1994 refit cover	*converted 2005/6 as Logos Hope*
Stena Sea Lynx/Stena Lynx	1993	Incat, Tasmania	1994/95/97/98	*in service 2004 as Mandarin in South Korea*
Vinzia E	1972	Rickmers, Bremerhaven Germany	1994 refit cover	*in service 2006 with Northlink Ferries as Clare*
Stena Sea Lynx II	1994	Incat, Tasmania	1994 emergency cover	*in service 2005 as Jaume*
Stena Antrim	1981	Harland & Wolff, Belfast	1995/6	*ex St Christopher. In service 2005 as Ibn Batouta*
Stena Londoner	1974	Brodogradiliste, Trogir, Yugoslavia	1996 refit cover	*4 weeks to 3.4.96. Scrapped 2005 as Volcan de Tacande*
Condor 10	1993	Incat, Tasmania	1996 season	*in service with Condor Ferries 2006*
Koningin Beatrix	1986	Van der Giessen-de Noord Rotterdam	1997 – 2002	*in service 2006 as Stena Baltica*
Stena Caledonia	1981	Harland & Wolff, Belfast	1998/99/05 refit cover	*ex St David [IV] - still in service ex Belfast 2006*
European Pathfinder	1975	Bremerhaven, Germany	13.07.98 only	***re-named** Begonia 2003 – Via Mare 2005*
Stena Lynx III	1996	Incat, Tasmania	Dec 98 onwards	*still in service*
Rosebay	1976	Hamburg, Germany	1999 refit cover	***re-named** Transparaden 2001 - Translandia 2004 - in service with Eckero Line*
Stena Invicta	1985	Nakskov, Denmark	2000 refit cover	*ex Peder Paars 1991 – Color Viking 2000 - in service 2005*
Stena Galloway	1980	Harland & Wolff, Belfast	2001 repair cover	*ex Galloway Princess – since 2002 Le Rif (IMTC Casablanca)*
Stena Europe	1981	Gotaverken Arendal, Gothenburg	2002 –	*in service 2006 on Fishguard – Rosslare route*
Stena Seafarer	1975	Hamburg, Germany	2006 refit cover	*in service 2006 on Fleetwood – Larne route*

STENA
FELICITY
STENA FELICITY
Sten

The **Stena Felicity** *leaving Fishguard during her last season on the route. (Miles Cowsill)*

ACKNOWLEDGEMENTS

The author would like to thank all those who have been involved with the production of this book. I am indebted to Eamonn Hewitt, Communications Manager (Irish Sea) Stena Line for his encouragement and enthusiasm with this centenary book and to my fellow colleagues, Dick Clague, Richard Kirkman, Martin Lewis, Robert Lloyd, John Maddock, Bernard Share and Gareth Williams, who have contributed to this title.

I am also grateful to the following who have assisted with photographs and other useful material for the book: Martin Lewis, Gordon Hislip, Mike O'Brian, Gregg Ryan, Dr David Jenkins & Kay Kays (National Museums & Galleries of Wales), Emma Challinor (Wirral Archives Services), Magdalena Mayo (NRM/ Science and Society Picture Library), FotoFlite, Justin Merrigan, David and Dorothy Parsons, Trevor Barrett, William Mayes, John Hendy, Clare Price and Pat Somner.

BIBLIOGRAPHY

Newport Pem. and Fishguard — Martin Lewis
Irish Passenger Steamship Services — D.B.McNeill
Railways and other Steamers — Duckworth & Langmuir
British Nationalised Shipping — Clegg and Styring
Sealink Years — Cowsill & Hendy
British Ferry Scene — Ferry Publications Ltd
European Ferry Scene — Ferry Publications Ltd
Sea Breezes
Western Telegraph
Sealink News

FERRY PUBLICATIONS

As specialists in this fascinating field of shipping, Miles Cowsill and John Hendy have, since founding Ferry Publications in 1987, produced a total range of publications covering all aspects of the ever-changing ferry scene in the North Sea, English Channel, Solent, Irish Sea, Scottish and now Scandinavian spheres of operations.

New titles and amended updates are constantly being produced or are in the planning stage. In order to keep up to date both with what is going on in the world of European ferries and with our new titles, we strongly recommended to subscribe to our quarterly magazine 'European Ferry Scene', which now also includes information on what's happening in Scandinavia and the Mediterranean.

Ferry Publications has gained a reputation for producing high quality books at very affordable prices. We pride ourselves in the standard of photographic reproduction which we achieve and we believe that our books fill a considerable gap in the market, not only for ship enthusiasts but also for anyone who has a passing interest in the ships and the sea.

For further information on Ferry Publication visit www.ferrypubs.co.uk

Stena Lynx III
LYNX
Stena Line